April 1984

$8^{\underline{45}}$

Growing Orchids
in Australia and New Zealand

Gordon C. Morrison

Kangaroo Press

INTRODUCTION

Possibly the introduction to a book is the hardest chapter to write. There is nothing before it and everything after it. So there is little to write about except the aims of the author to be expressed in the text and the intended purpose of the book.

Firstly this is not meant to be a scientific treatise, far from it in fact, for so many technical facts have been jumped over in order to keep the text to a size within the publisher's limits. It is however, a modest attempt at being a text book on some aspects of orchid culture, aspects which are important to both the newcomer and to the longer term grower.

In several respects it differs from many orchid books on the market. The most obvious is that it is not a picture book as such, but rather it contains information on plant culture, set down, hopefully, in a manner which is meaningful to produce understanding rather than just knowledge.

Secondly the text has been divided into three sections: the Chapters, the Topics and the Appendices.

It is not realistic to say that the Chapters are for newcomers and the Topics for the experienced and the Appendices for both, but this was the basic idea. It is, of course, quite impossible to draw a clear cut line between these two groups. Some newcomers to orchid culture are experienced plantsmen of many years standing and are hardly neophytes. Others of long standing in the matter of orchid culture can well appreciate some of the basic plant talk which does not dwell on how large the flowers are or how many flowers there should be on a stem. So there is a large grey area on both sides of the line and it is hoped that all readers will benefit from the text. Newcomers can stop whenever bewilderment sets in and as experience grows so that the subject becomes more relevant and understandable so the book again serves to instruct and inform.

The Topics are meant to be self-contained, that is each refers to one subject only but this does not mean that material contained in the Chapters is not relevant to the Topic. The Chapters come first, the Topics second if a broad spectrum outline of the subject is desired.

When writing both Chapters and Topics a pause is made here and there to make a comment, perhaps irrelevant to the subject, perhaps not, but it may spur the reader to undertake further reading and research into plants and orchids in particular.

In Chapter 5 the plan is to deal with the anatomy of the orchid plant. Line drawings or even pictures need to be supported by some explanation but irrespective of the quality of the drawings, there is nothing as informative as dissecting the plant itself, or at least inspecting a live plant with a hand lens. Magnifications up to $10 \times$ are quite adequate to see the detail of the anther cap and to remove the pollinia and observe the sticky stigma.

As in all progressive technology, orchid growing is not static, that which was learned this year needs to be updated next year. After this basic text has been digested the orchidologist needs to refer to periodicals and to facilitate a choice, a list of these is given in Appendix 3, with a comment on the nature and value of each.

On page 79 there is a Glossary which is not meant to be exhaustive and explain all the terms used in orchidology. However it should provide sufficient help for the reader of this book.

Acknowledgments

The author is indebted to Mr. P. Collin for the loan of photograph for Fig. 1-1 and colour plates 10, 21, 22, 23, and 24, and to Mr. L. Brunckhorst for technical assistance in the preparation of Figs. 5-6 A,B,C.

The author is indebted to Mr. J.J. Betts for his painstaking perusal of the manuscript and for many useful suggestions which have been incorporated into the text.

Cover picture: *Paraphalaenopsis denevei* (J.J. Sm.) A.D. Hawkes, a rare plant from Kalimantan photographed in the author's glasshouse in December 1981. This species was discovered in 1925.

First published in 1982 by
Kangaroo Press
3 Whitehall Road, Kenthurst 2154
Typeset by G.T. Setters Pty Limited
Printed in Hong Kong by Colorcraft Ltd

ISBN 0 949924 27 X

CONTENTS

Introduction   2

Chapters

  1. Distribution, Diversity & Ecology   4
  2. The Orchid Family   11
  3. Purchasing Plants   14
  4. Housing Plants   16
  5. Anatomy of Orchids   19
  6. Substrates and Culture   23
  7. The Naming of Hybrids   30
  8. Description of Plants   49
  9. Propagation—Sexual & Asexual   52
 10. Deflasking and Community Pots   56
 11. Pests and Diseases   58

Colour Plates

Topics

  1. The Glasshouse   62
  2. Importing Orchids & Quarantine   66
  3. Mycorrhizal Associations   67
  4. Carbon Fixation   69
  5. Taxonomy & Nomenclature   72
  6. An Electronic Thermostat for the Glasshouse   73

Appendices

  1. Sun Tables   76
  2. Technical Data   76
  3. Further Reading   78
  4. Glossary   79

Index   80

1. THE DISTRIBUTION, DIVERSITY & ECOLOGY OF ORCHIDS

The above title may be translated to read—Orchids, where do they grow, how different are they and how do they fit into their environment? Altogether a large subject but one which forms an effective introduction to this large family. Further it is a subject which is usually acquired only by enthusiastic and experienced orchid growers over a long period of time. Therefore, a short dissertation on the subject should be a useful introduction and experience for both the newcomer to orchid growing and to those growers who have found it difficult to gain this information.

If there is one clear dividing line in the orchid family relevant to all three subjects of the chapter heading it is geophytes versus epiphytes. That is orchids which grow in the ground versus orchids which grow on trees or rocks. The fact that rock growing types may sometimes be called lithophytes is not significant to this subject so is not taken into account in this chapter. '-phyte and phyto-' come from the Greek 'phyton' meaning plant and are used extensively as a suffix and prefix in botanical and horticultural texts.

The dividing line is not sharp as several orchids which grow in the ground will, in culture, grow quite well in substrates other than soil. Also some apparently geophytic orchids are really growing in leaf mould and not in the soil proper. So one has to draw a line with some grey areas on each side to accommodate these various possibilities but this is usual in biological considerations. Biology, unlike physics, is not a clear cut subject and shades of grey are universal.

Nevertheless, separation into geophytes (sometimes called terrestrial) and epiphytes is a convenient one for our purpose here and it can well be applied to other considerations in the orchid field. For example, in respect of distribution, it is usual to find epiphytes diminish with increasing latitude, both north and south. By way of illustration using Australian native orchids, Queensland has 136 epiphytes compared with 48 in N.S.W. and 2 in Tasmania. Geophytes usually show the opposite trend, although some areas, centrally located climatically, seem to favour orchid growth in general. Compared with 134 geophytes in Queensland there are 182 in N.S.W. and 116 in Tasmania.

In themselves these figures are not very meaningful but if turned into percentage values of the total orchids native to a State the result is much more obvious.

State	Epiphytes	Geophytes
Queensland	50%	50%
N.S.W.	21%	79%
Tasmania	2%	98%

This shows clearly how epiphytes dominate in lower latitudes where the weather is essentially tropical and geophytes dominate in the higher latitudes where it is often cold and the weather varies a great deal between summer and winter. It is, of course, unrealistic biologically to use State boundaries which are not respected by plant growth. However, plant data are usually compiled on the basis of political boundaries such as 'Flora of Columbia' and 'Flora of Brazil', the separation between the two simply being a line drawn on a map and quite unrealistic for the separation of growth areas for any particular species.

A similar trend exists in the northern hemisphere, the orchids of Europe are of the geophytic type.

Although the Evolution or Origin of the orchids is relevant to the title of this chapter it is not dealt with here to any extent, being too voluminous and complex and too subject to expert disagreement to spoil an interesting chapter. However, the mention of a few factors of origin is worthwhile to assist the explanation of distribution.

The family of orchids is believed to have originated in the floristic area of Malesia, specifically east Malesia. This latter is an area created and designated as a floristic region to overcome the occurrence of species on both sides of a political border. It incorporates such political areas as peninsular Malaysia, Sumatra, Borneo and the Philippines. The area of Malesia is the site of many famous 'biological lines' such as the Wallace Line and the Zollinger Line, drawn to separate clearly different fauna and flora zones. These need not concern us here except to reinforce the concept that many plant families may have originated in areas which we now know as South-East Asia and dispersed from here to other parts of the world. It is this distribution which forms part of this chapter.

Notwithstanding the very large number of genera in the Orchidaceae only some 32 of these have had so-called trans-Oceanic distribution and 27 of these are exclusively geophytes (Garay, Proceedings of

4th World Orchid Conference). This appears to indicate that dispersal took place early in the life of a family perhaps before the continents as we know them, drifted apart. The geophytic orchid is regarded as being more primitive than the epiphyte, a point which will be covered later in the chapter.

Continental drift is now a well established concept of Geology (since 1967) even though it was proposed in 1912. The theory is that originally the land mass of the earth formed one single continent called 'Pangaea'. This split into two parts, 'Laurasia' in the north and 'Gondwanaland' in the south. Both of these latter split further, or in some cases joined up with other masses, to form the continents we know today. However, before this splitting took place both fauna and flora were able to migrate across land surfaces (e.g. Africa was joined to South America), rather than across oceans. Transoceanic migrations, although not impossible have always worried biologists.

In 1883 a volcanic eruption occurred on the island of Krakatao in Indonesia and all vegetation was destroyed, so the re-vegetation process was of significant interest to warrant investigation and observation. In 1896 three orchids were found growing on the island, these were *Spathoglottis plicata*, *Arundina speciosa* and *Cymbidium finlaysonianum*, all geophytes. The first epiphyte was a fern found in 1906. By 1928 the epithytes had increased to 23, 13 of which were orchids and by 1933 the orchids had increased to 17 epiphytic and 18 geophytic species.

Krakatao Island has Sumatra to the west and Java to the east, both comparatively large islands, the latter having some 900 orchid species so, until 1933 Krakatao had not 'caught' many orchid seeds. As a general rule, the smaller the land mass the smaller the diversity of natural flora but this is modified by distance over water and by man. The Hawaiian Islands have a reasonably poor native flora with only three species of orchids. These islands are of volcanic origin and as far as is known have always been a great distance from any land mass. Early man is also thought to have contributed substantially to plant dispersal, particularly in respect of those plants of medicinal use, taking these from island to island as new settlements were made. Orchids could have been included, as many of these contain alkaloids, substances which have a physiological effect on the human body. This interference by early man in plant distribution has caused plants to appear in places where plant geographers would not expect them to occur.

In order for an orchid seed to germinate in the wild it needs a suitable resting place or substrate upon which to grow but in addition it needs a mycorrhizal fungus to supply its initial needs. See Topic 3 for a detailed account of this subject. This fungus must have also been transported to Krakatao and one wonders how this happened in such a short space of time and how the fungus arrived at the same place as the orchid seed. In this respect it is worth noting that some 30 years after the volcanic eruption (i.e. 1913) 30 species of land and freshwater birds were again inhabiting the island.

This author has long supported the concept that birds, which are very mobile, are both terrestrial and arboreal and which have separate nesting and feeding grounds are responsible for the dispersal of both orchid seed and its necessary fungus. Feathers, hair, wool, hoofs, nails are made from a group of fibrous proteins called Keratins and when dry this protein can develop an electrostatic charge, e.g. the crackling of dry hair when combed. The preening of bird feathers may likewise develop an electrostatic charge and pick up and retain orchid seeds for transport to another place, e.g. a nesting site or a feeding site. Orchid seeds, being very small, will respond quite aggressively to the proximity of a charged surface and adhere thereto. Given a time scale of something like a million years (a megayear) the bird–orchid seed transfer rate would not need to be very great to ensure a progressive transfer of seed (and of fungus) over at least hundreds of kilometres, extending by steps to thousands of kilometres. As environment changed so the birds would gradually migrate to new areas or extend their own populations taking orchid seeds and fungus particles with them.

The apparent ability of geophytes to migrate more readily than epiphytes may be attributed to the greater probability of the mycorrhizal fungus being present in soil rather than on the bark of a tree. In fact some barks produce phenolic exudates which could well be inhibitory to fungal growth which may explain why orchid seeds do not germinate on some trees while on adjacent trees of a different species they grow prolifically.

Orchid dispersal or distribution is world-wide, species occurring in all areas except the Arctic and Antarctic. Recently an orchid, *Corybas macranthus* (naturally a geophyte) was discovered on Macquarie Island which places the distribution closer to the Antarctic than previously suspected.

Diversity

Although most orchid flowers have a similar basic arrangement in the flower of three sepals and three petals, one petal being highly modified to form a lip or labellum (see chapter on Anatomy) the appearance of the flowers is very different over the estimated 750 genera. In fact there is no other plant family so florally diversified as to size, shape, colour, arrangement, scents and pollinators.

In addition to flower form there are many different vegetative forms. There is the 'bull-rush' type of leaf as in the *Cymbidium*, the 'aspidistra' type of leaf as in some *Coelogyne*, the 'heart' leaf as in *Corybas*, the 'rod-like' leaves of several species, the thick fleshy and sometimes knobbly leaves of some *Dendrobium* species and there are many others including 'no-leaves-at-all' type.

The flower recognised by most people as an orchid is typified by the 'florists delight', the *Cymbidium* or *Cattleya* flower, large and showy. It is significant that large showy flowers are usually favoured even by orchid growers when selecting a winner for the 'popular vote' at orchid society meetings. However, there are other types of orchid flowers, not only differing in size but also in shape.

Perhaps the best known is the so-called 'slipper orchid' of which four genera are recognised, all belonging to the sub-family Cypripedioideae (see Chapter 2 on the Orchid Family for a description of these names). One genus of this type grows naturally in some northern countries, such as in Europe, Japan and North America, as a geophyte and represents to the inhabitants of these countries the typical orchid form.

Another type, represented by the sub-family Apostasioideae, is not always recognised as an orchid on initial examination. There are only two genera and sixteen species all regarded as primitive orchids but not the ancestors of those we regard as evolutionary more advanced. It is probably that, like so many 'odd-ball' plant species of limited numbers, the species of this sub-family side-stepped out of the evolutionary stream and remained primitive through millions of years. The genera are *Apostasia* and *Neuwiedia*; they are strictly of botanical interest and will not be included elsewhere in this text.

Also of botanical interest and listed here to illustrate extreme diversity are those orchids which grow underground and are saprophytic, that is they do not make their own foodstuffs from carbon dioxide and water, using energy from sunlight. Of the sub-terranian types one grows in New South Wales (*Cryptanthemis slateri*) the other in Western Australia (*Rhizanthella gardneri*) and a third in New Zealand (*Corybas cryptanthus*). *Rhizanthella gardneri* spends its entire life below the surface of the ground. At the opening of the flower bud a small hole is formed in the surface of the soil by the bracts so that the flower is exposed to the air but the flower stalk does not extend to push the flower upwards.

While the above species do not photosynthesise by using energy from sunlight there are other orchids with no leaves at all. These use their roots to absorb nutrients like any other plant and at the same time overcome distance transport problems by also using the roots to absorb carbon dioxide. The roots contain the green chlorophyll to absorb light energy and convert the carbon dioxide and water into sugars. These sugars act as food and by combining with other absorbed nutrients provide all the materials needed for plant growth. One such genus is *Taeniophyllum*, four species of which occur in Australia.

Australia has two of the smallest orchids known, *Bulbophyllum globuliforme* and *B. minutissimum*, the former having pseudobulbs only 1–2 mm in diameter but the flowers in the latter are the smaller of the two species being about 3–4 mm across. On the other side of the scale *Grammatophyllum speciosum* has thick stems some 4.5 metres long with an inflorescence (flower head) some 2 metres long with many 10 cm wide flowers. This plant occurs from Sumatra to the Philippines.

Pollination

The diversity of pollination methods in orchids is a study in itself and only a few examples are possible here. Apart from a few species which are self pollinating (autogamous) most of the transferring of pollen from one flower to the stigma of another is done by insects of some type, usually bees, flies, gnats, wasps and moths.

In most cases when we speak of pollen from an orchid we mean the pollen mass or pollinium (pl. pollinia) which is usually contained at the top of a structure called the column. The pollinia are housed under a small cap at the top of the column while the sticky stigmatic surface which leads to the plant ovary is located lower down on the column. (Refer to the chapter on plant anatomy.) The pollinia are often carried on short stalks at the base of which is a sticky disc which adheres to the insect. One of the most intriguing facets of pollination is the way the flowers, or their parts, arrange for the visiting pollen laden insect to direct the pollen mass into the flower stigma.

The mechanism of *Orchis mascula*, common in England is a good example. A bumble bee lands on the lip and tries to obtain nectar from a long spur in the flower. His head touches the base of the pollinia and the sticky discs adhere to his head and the glue sets hard and dry. It takes about 30 seconds for a bee to fly from one flower, find another and enter. During this period the stalk carrying the pollinia has bent forward through an angle of 45°

so it is now 45° to the bee's head in just the ideal position to ram the pollen into the stigma of the next flower visited. The stigma is sticky and retains some of the pollinia with sufficient force, that on departure of the bee, elastic threads holding the stuck pollinia break away from the main mass. The bee is then free to continue to another flower and pollinate it. This is not the end of the story for if the area or season should be a little short on the correct type of bee, the pollinia stalks collapse. Instead of holding the pollinia upright it now dangles down in front of the stigma so any disturbance, such as wind or another insect will swing the pollinia against the sticky stigma and self pollination occurs, not the best method but better than no pollination at all for the survival of the species.

In order to attract insects the flower must promise the insect some reward or encouragement. In the above example the reward was nectar but some orchids produce a sugar/starch substance from the callus on the lip, this is known as pseudopollen or false pollen and is used by the insect as a food source.

Advertising that sex is available is another method used by orchids to attract the males of the pollination species. Species of the genus *Ophrys* have evolved flowers which give off a pheromone, a chemical substance or combination of substances, which influence the behaviour of animals of a single species (usually). This pheromone is often a sex attractant detected by males which flock to the plant anxious to copulate.

The male adult insects emerge from their pupal stage some weeks earlier than females and seem most anxious to prove themselves as soon as possible with anything that resembles the female of the species. In this process of pseudocopulation the pollinia are removed and deposited on another flower of the same species.

Many Australian geophytic species in the genera *Cryptostylis*, *Caladenia*, *Calochilus*, *Chiloglottis*, *Drakea* and *Thelymitra* offer pseudocopulation to a variety of flies, gnats, bees and wasps.

Apparently humans were not the first organisms to get drunk! Orchids of the genera *Coryanthes*, *Gongora* and *Stanhopea* offer intoxicating fluids to their pollinating bees. In *Coryanthes*, for example, the visiting bees are attracted to a special tissue containing intoxicating fluid, situated at the base of the lip. The bees scratch this tissue to release a fluid which affects their sense organs, they lose their grip and fall into a bucket formed by the lip. This bucket contains a 'soapy' water and it takes the bee some 15 to 30 minutes to escape by a passage-way thoughtfully provided by the orchid flower. In this process it picks up pollinia. The bee is firstly at-

tracted by the scent but as soon as the pollinia is removed the scent disappears so the bee does not again enter that flower, an arrangement to prevent self pollination.

Fascinating as this subject is, this is not a chapter on pollination and the foregoing must serve to illustrate a little of the diversity of orchids. It is just one of the attractive subjects open to those who take an interest in orchid culture and desire to know how things happen in nature.

Ecology

The terms Ecology, Ecosystems and Environment have been promoted in recent years to embrace many facets of our lives. Some aspects have been highly emotive, others have been purely factual and scientific. The remainder of this chapter is devoted to how orchids may profit or suffer from their environment and a final comment is made on conservation of the species.

In general orchids are stress-tolerant plants, as are many plants which have had to live in and endure harsh conditions. Those ancestors of our present species, which possessed some genetic twist that enabled them to survive while others of their race perished have, over millions of years produced populations in tune with the environment. As the environment changed, e.g. during the ice age, so those plants genetically equipped to withstand the changes, survived, others perished. The survivors produced a new population of the species which may have been intolerant of further changes and so perished or formed new populations from isolated survivors. We must not assume that the orchids we know today were all present in the origin of the family or that those orchids which were ancestors of today's plants are themselves currently in existence.

It is important to note that the genotype of the plant and not the phenotype (which is influenced by the environment) determines its survival under changing conditions. That is, the genetic make up of the plant held in its chromosomes determines its response to changing environments and whether it will survive or not. If it survives then a new population is formed by its progeny, a population perhaps slightly different from its ancestral type. Repeat this over millions of years and new species are formed.

The phenotype of the plant is not inheritable. That is, if a plant is taken from the field and grown under improved conditions it will look to be a better plant and may even flower much more prolifically than its brothers in the field. The reason may be simple—more water, more fertiliser. Every orchid grower who has jungle-collected plants transferred to his glasshouse is aware of this. The poor, stressed, insect eaten, fungus-blotched plants take on a new lease of life yet this improvement (in the phenotypic plant) is not inheritable. Its progeny will be just as poor as the parent if transferred to the wild. Inheritance is a one way ticket—from DNA in the chromosomes outwards—never in the reverse direction.

Nevertheless, it has been a doctrine among orchid growers that a study of the natural environment of a plant is helpful in establishing the desired conditions for cultivation of the plant. This was well demonstrated in England in the 1800s when orchids imported from the tropics were killed when housed under hot dry conditions. The collectors omitted to advise the growers of the local prevailing conditions, so the plants, being from the tropics, were placed in a 'hot house' or 'stove house' as it was then called. No doubt the above doctrine has its roots embedded in such occurrences.

While an investigation of the local growing conditions of the plant is highly desirable it is fallacious to consider these to be optimum and which must, at all costs, be reproduced. The plant will usually respond quite well to any conditions imposing less stress on it.

There are various types of stress brought about by nature and mankind. In the wild the most common are water stress, nutrient stress and light stress. Mankind contributes stress to populations by chopping down trees in the forest and by bulldozing the land to dig holes in it or plant crops to feed his never ending proliferation of progeny.

Some orchids are opportunists, taking advantage of this disturbance in much the same way as weeds populate and proliferate in disturbed areas. One has only to look at the *Arundina graminifolia* (**Plate 2**) growing on the grass covered hillsides of Malaysia. It grows only in these open sunny places, never in forests, so in the remote past it must have been a comparatively rare plant which has multiplied following disturbance of the land. There are other opportunist orchids including *Spathoglottis*, *Phaius*, and *Epidendrum* species.

As tropical epiphytic orchids seem to be the major interest of collectors most of this chapter will be devoted to their ecology. Table 1 sets down the advantages and disadvantages of an epiphytic existence compared to life growing in the soil (geophytic).

Earlier in this chapter, when dealing with distribution, it was stated that some trees do not support an orchid population possibly because phenolic exudates inhibit fungal growth. This inhibition can also extend to the growth of lichens (a fungal–algal combination). There are some orchid

seeds which will germinate only on lichens and not on the bark. At this point some differentiation must be made between germination and growth. Adult plants, as distinct from seeds and seedlings, will grow on almost any tree which does not shed its bark, so it is really germination of the seed in the wild which is ecologically important for the perpetuation of the species.

The fruit of an orchid plant is called a capsule and it produces vast quantities of seed, not all of it being viable. A fruit of a *Cycnoches* species may contain three million seeds while the fruit of a *Cypripedium* contains only about 28 000 seeds. Naturally with such large numbers the seeds must be very tiny. A typical seed is pictured in **Fig. 1-1**

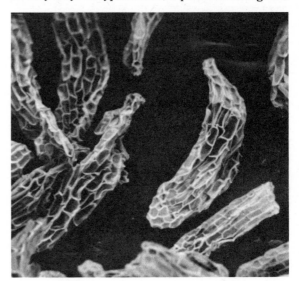

Fig. 1-1   Orchid seed × 140

which was taken with a Scanning Electron Microscope. The length is about 400 micrometres and the width 100 micrometres. The actual growing part, called the protoembryo is much smaller, being encased in the mesh-like structure of the seed. The weight of a typical seed is three micrograms and is readily blown over considerable distances to lodge in bark crevices, humus clumps in tree forks and is caught by lichens and mosses growing on tree branches. The habitat for germination provided by mosses sometimes results in epiphytes being found in the damp moss covered ground if the situation has sufficient light for orchid growth.

Many orchids have adapted to water stress conditions or perhaps it would be better to say that those orchids which have adapted to water stress are still living. A plant is passive and environmental decision-making attributes to improve its lot in life must not be given to it or assumed. Those plants which have the equipment to survive in dry conditions will live if dry conditions prevail, the plants without such equipment will die out. Humans, by growing plants in a greenhouse can modify the environment to relieve water stress but this can be overdone resulting in the death and debilitation of many plants. This is a human failure experienced by many beginners in orchid culture when trying to grow epiphytic orchids in pots. It is difficult to find a potted plant in the jungle!

The greatest number of epiphytes are found where there is ample rainfall of 50 to 75 mm per month. Many are found at altitudes of 1500 metres or more where mist or clouds cover the trees every night. During the author's stay in Cibodas (Java) at an altitude of 1400 metres it rained regularly each day from 4 to 4.30 pm and in the mountains of Malaysia at 1500 metres the cloud cover drifted over regularly an hour or so before sunset, bathing the tree tops in moisture.

At lower altitudes many orchids depend on rivers and waterfalls to maintain high humidity. The water storage ability of some lower altitude orchids, e.g. *Phalaenopsis* is minimal so frequent rain and continuously high humidity is a necessity. In cultivation, a desiccated *Phalaenopsis* is a sorry sight when the glasshouse humidity has been allowed to fall too low for too long a period. At these lower altitudes many orchids grow on tree branches along the edge of a river. Not only is high humidity maintained but the light penetrates to a greater extent than in the denser forest. In cultivation many orchids thrive in a situation which simulates a river. Good unimpeded air flow over moist stones with a dense creeper as the backdrop and very light shading over the top simulates a stream in your own yard.

Epiphytic orchids have a very specialised root system wherein the actively conducting part of the root is covered with many layers of spongy cellular material called the velamen. This material is very water absorbent and it has the great merit of catching the first rain water dripping from the leaves of the supporting tree. This water is rich in minerals absorbed by the tree roots from the soil and exuded on to the leaf surface, to be washed downwards by the rain. This process is called leaching and nutrients are cycled from plant to plant or plant to soil by this method. Elements necessary for plant growth which are leached are sodium, manganese, calcium, magnesium, potassium, iron and phosphorus. In addition to these some sugars are leached, together with plant growth substances surplus to the tree. Leaching from the older leaves is greater than from young leaves which absorb the substances readily for their own growth, whereas the cells of the older leaves have less requirement for rapid absorption and even excrete some of their unwanted sugars to the intercellular spaces from which leaching occurs.

For some reason this source of nutrients receives little mention in orchid texts which prefer to rely on decomposing leaves and bird droppings as the source of nutrition. In the jungles birds are not so prolific as that and although birds may contribute, along with other arboreal animals, this amount of nutrient would not feed many plants.

The rainfall does not have to be heavy to cause leaching, in fact dew and a continuous light drizzle are more effective than heavy rain. The surface of the leaf only needs to be wetted and the leaves of many tropical rain forest trees have a 'drip-tip' at their far end to collect surface water and drip this off the leaf. Of course orchids are plants and as far as is known also suffer from leaching so that growers who regularly mist their plants need to apply fertiliser fairly frequently if the plants are growing in a house. Other aspects of ecology are covered in the Topic 4 on carbon fixation, a subject too extensive in its range to be included here.

Comment on orchid ecology would not be complete without mention of the saprophytic orchids. This latter term is used for plants which do not photosynthesise or manufacture their own food but rather live on dead organic material aided by root inhabiting fungi. Good examples of this are seen in the genus *Galeola* two species of which are in Australia. These are *G. cassythoides* and *G. foliata* neither of which has leaves but climb up forest trees to a reported height of 4.5 metres or even higher to 15 metres for the latter species. They rely partly on decomposed bark for sustenance and cultivation is well nigh impossible away from their natural habitat.

Another Australian saprophyte is *Dipodium punctatum*, a rather beautiful geophyte which many people have dug up in a fruitless attempt to cultivate it. In the bush it is found closely associated with eucalypts but then, where in the southern Australian bush, is it devoid of eucalypts? So the association may only be assumed and not confirmed, however, the assumption appears reasonably possible.

The flowering period of orchids is usually controlled by both light and temperature in various ways and combinations. As the pollination of orchids is rather dependent on the correct species of insect being present, survival of the species is dependent on flowering being coincident with the arrival on the scene of the adult insect. By flowering during different periods of the year related species may occupy the same geographical area without hybridising naturally. This hybridisation may also be avoided by each orchid species having its own specific pollinator, being constructed to facilitate entry of that insect and excluding others. From the insect's point of view this must have some advantage as it ensures that insect a source of food which is denied to others and so reduces the competition.

Conservation

For many years some orchidologists have been concerned with the mass removal or destruction of orchid species growing in their natural habitat. Removal is for two reasons: (a) the collector is an orchid grower and takes only a few plants for his own use from the crop; or (b) the collector has a market for as many plants as he can obtain. This may be for an overseas nursery, for a local nursery (which in turn probably supplies the overseas customer) or for sale to individuals in the street or at the so-called native market.

For example, in Sabah and similar places it is quite easy to buy orchids from street hawkers. When the money to buy tomorrow's food is represented by an orchid crop the collector must be biased towards his own existence.

The major destruction is by logging or forest clearing to grow crops to feed the ever increasing human population. In most countries the orchids (and other plants) are burnt in the logged areas because the authorities do not seem to be aware that such plants may be dollar earners if collected and sold to overseas markets.

This is rather surprising as 69 countries are signatories to the Convention on Trade in Endangered Species of fauna and flora (CITES). This Convention was principally organised by zoologists and intended for fauna protection but plants were lumped in at the end, whole families of them including orchids.

This is obviously ridiculous as many orchid species have no real commercial value. A study of a catalogue of a leading U.S.A. Orchid nursery shows 316 species listed for sale from all over the world. This is 1.6% of the estimated number of species so that most orchid species will never be endangered by collectors, they will disappear under the blade of the bulldozer. Of course, this does not mean that orchid fanciers are limited to, or would limit themselves to this 1.6%, nevertheless, it would indeed take an ardent and rich collector to reach 10% of the total number of species.

In the U.S.A. the Customs Authority is apparently implementing the Convention with zeal as all plants imported and not covered by the necessary and complex paper work are confiscated and sent to a 'rescue centre' to care for these. This seldom functions and many plants are destroyed in the name of conservation. It is a peculiar world!

Some countries have realised that orchids are a dollar crop for the population and collection is restricted to indigenous persons who may then sell to foreign growers at a price fair to both. This is a small scale affair but is an income source of a modest amount for those trained in orchid collection. It is a pity more countries do not help their indigenes in this manner.

Table 1

The advantages and disadvantages of an epiphytic existence compared with a geophytic existence

Advantages

1. Little competition in the tree tops except from ferns and bromeliads.

2. Ready availability of pollinators.

3. Better seed dispersal by wind.

4. Freedom from ground chewers, e.g. snails and herbivores.

5. Higher light intensity as only a few orchids are shade tolerant.

6. Good air movement to improve carbon dioxide concentration around leaf and prevent fungal spores depositing on leaf. Also helps keep plant cool.

Disadvantages

1. Possible water stress in dry areas.

2. Limited minerals available for nutrition.

3. Less chance of seed falling in suitable spot for germination. Some trees antagonistic to germination.

4. Less chance of suitable mycorrhizal fungus being present.

2. THE ORCHID FAMILY

One of the most important sub-divisions of the Plant Kingdom is the Family and all plants are classified as belonging to a given Family. In rare cases, if a new plant does not fit into any existing Family then a new one is created for it.

Orchids are no exception and all fit into the family called Orchidaceae (pronounced Or-kid-ace-ee-ee). There has been some attempt at times to split off some orchids and place them in other families but this has not gained favour with recognised orchid taxonomists both in England and the United States of America. A taxonomist is a botanist specialising in the classification of plants. The families are themselves grouped into other larger sub-divisions and while they are not of great importance to the culture of orchid plants it is of interest to see how orchids are related to other plants.

Firstly orchids have water conducting pipes in the stems and leaves as have most other plants. This separates them from algae and mosses which must rely on the slow diffusion of water through the plant which can grow only to a limited height unless totally immersed in water. The pipe lines allow some plants to grow to great heights, as the forest giants and even some orchids have stems from 3 to 4.5 metres long.

Orchids and many other plants produce fruits containing seeds and this property separates them from Ferns, which do not produce seeds and Conifers (cone bearing plants) where the seeds are not confined to a seed case. The next sub-division is the Class in which plants are classified as either Dicotyledons or Monocotyledons according to whether the seed contains two or one seed leaf respectively. However, of greater interest to the gardener are two other properties of the Classes.

Dicotyledons have flower segments in fours or fives and have cambial tissue which, each year, increases the girth of the plant stem. This is an obvious characteristic of trees but it occurs, perhaps to a less obvious extent, in other plants which survive for more than a year. The Monocotyledons (which includes the orchids) have flower segments in threes and no cambium tissue to increase the stem size over the first year's growth. For example, *Dendrobium* stems reach maximum size during their first year due to cellular proliferation and expansion but then stabilise at the end of the growing season and remain stable until they finally shrink and die.

Gardeners who tie plants (in the dicot. Class) to stakes will be aware that permanent (e.g. metal) ties need to be loosened each year to avoid damage to the stem. No such action is needed with Monocot. stems.

The Classes are then divided into Orders which are largely of academic interest and of little practical value to the gardener so will not be discussed further.

The next sub-division is the Family which is of interest to the gardener as it helps to associate one species of plant with another. Typically we have the Daisy Family, the Rose Family, the Geranium Family, the Grass Family, the Legume Family all with their proper botanical names. Of the flowering plant families Orchidaceae is the largest having at least 20 000 species (some consider the figure to be larger). This is followed by the Compositae (Daisy) with 13 000 species; Leguminosae with 12 000 species; Gramineae (Grass) with 10 000 species. One of the smallest families is Calycanthaceae with only seven species. These large numbers of species are, of course, estimates in round figures as the views and opinions of various taxonomists differ and with reclassifications occurring, the exact number of species is difficult to determine.

In the Orchidaceae it is not clear whether some of the plants bear two names, so the counting of herbarium specimens without a careful analysis of each does not result in an exact figure. Additionally, no one herbarium contains all species of orchids. Also taxonomists are continuing to raise varieties to the rank of species and to derate some species to varietal rank of other species so the whole process is in a state of flux.

Having accepted that the Orchidaceae is the highest level of classification of use to orchid growers it is then pertinent to consider lower levels of classification totally within the Family. The level below Family is Sub-family which is logical enough and of importance.

In the classification system proposed by Robert L. Dressler six sub-families are named. This classification system will be used throughout this book except that Dr Dressler (personal communication) has, in the light of further evidence, now grouped his proposed Vandoideae into Epidendroideae, making a total of five sub-families as follows.

	Pronounced
Apostasioideae	Arp-oh-stace-ee-oy-dee-ee
Cypripedioideae	Sip-rip-eed-ee-oy-dee-ee
Orchidoideae	Orchid-oy-dee-ee
Spiranthoideae	Spire-anth-oy-dee-ee
Epidendroideae	Epee-dend-roy-dee-ee

It is true that some classical Latin scholars may not agree with the pronounciation given above, nevertheless this is as used by botanists and orchid growers so will be understood. It is worth noting here that family names end in -aceae. There is currently a move to change those which do not so end to make these conform. Similarly sub-family names end in -oideae. This makes it entirely unnecessary to precede these names with the words family or sub-family as the endings make this evident.

The level of classification below Sub-family is 'Tribe'. This is of major interest as it indicates to some extent the ability of orchids within a Tribe to cross-breed and form a hybrid plant even though such a plant may itself be sterile. Dressler has proposed 21 Tribes for the Orchidaceae which is more than hitherto used. Other large families such as the Gramineae has 19 Tribes and the Leguminosae has 25 Tribes. Given the large size of the Orchidaceae and its very wide variation of growth habit, flower shape and reproductive organs it does not seem unreasonable to have five Sub-families and 21 Tribes. As more chemical and anatomical information comes to hand about orchid plants the classification system will, no doubt, be further modified.

In this book each genus described (other than hybrids) will be allocated to a Tribe and a lower level of classification, the Sub-tribe, to give a better understanding of the relationship between genera. This procedure is seldom done with other families as the species are so few that the generic level is sufficient and Tribes and Sub-tribes, if they exist, are not of any great significance. Many old-time orchid growers will assert that they grow orchids and take prizes without ever having heard of Tribes or Sub-tribes. This is quite so and not everyone needs this knowledge, particularly if one's entire ambition is limited to winning prizes with hybrids at shows. However, there is a lot more to orchid culture than this, as articles in good orchid journals will demonstrate. It is for those who wish to follow these articles and understand more about the subject than just winning prizes, that this book is written.

The next level below Sub-tribe is the genus (pl. genera) and like the other levels of classification, there are similarities between members of the level. For example, as stated previously the level of 'Class' separates those plants having 4/5 flower segments

and cambium tissue from those having 3 flower segments and no cambium tissue. Each time we drop down one level in classification so the gap between the plants comprising that level becomes narrower. At the generic level the members of the genus usually have well recognisable characteristics although some may not be obvious without a closer look. For example, the two genera, *Laelia* and *Cattleya* may be confused until one counts the number of pollinia present (see chapter on anatomy). One type of *Dendrobium* may be mistaken for a *Coelogyne* until one examines the pollinia. In general both the vegetative characteristics and the reproductive anatomy (flowers, pollinia and ovary) are factors which characterise a genus. Most *Dendrobium* species have thin stems with a girth from 4 mm to 90 mm but there is one section of the genus having flattened V shaped leaves so that, unless aware of this variation, one may not initially recognise the plant as a *Dendrobium*.

The next levels down are Sub-genera and Sections but skip these for a moment and go to the next level of species (pl. species). Note that the singular is not 'specie' which means 'coin of the realm'. This is the basic level of plant classification, not necessarily the lowest level but that which is of major concern in classification and often the most difficult and arguable.

The word 'species' has no special connotation. In Latin it simply means 'kind'. The many groups of kinds of organisms are called species. As mentioned previously the number of species recognisable in a family or a genus is often difficult to assess as various taxonomists have their own ideas on just what differences are worthy of classifying plants within or not within a given species. This can even extend to genera when some taxonomists consider a special feature or features warrants separation, e.g. *Paraphalaenopsis* separated out from *Phalaenopsis*.

A definition of species is difficult, although all taxonomists claim to recognise a species, few will define it. Three definitions are given here to give some idea of the concept.
1. Groups of actually or potentially interbreeding natural populations which are reproductively isolated from other such groups.
2. A naturally occurring collection of plants which can interbreed in nature and bear a resemblance to each other.
3. A group of plants showing intergradation among its individuals and having in common one or more characteristics which definitely separate it from any other group, i.e. it is distinct from other kinds.

Note that definition 3 avoids any reference to interbreeding. Orchids are such promiscuous plants that interbreeding is possible, not only at specific level but also at generic level. In nature such interbreeding between species is prevented only by physical barrier separation or difference in flowering time. Some authors attribute this promiscuity to the hypothesis that orchids are very recent in plant evolution and the species have not yet stabilised.

In some genera, e.g. *Dendrobium*, the number of species is so large and the characteristics so varied that the genus is divided into Sections, some 33 Sections or more in all (although some of doubtful validity) and species allocated to these Sections. In classical taxonomy the flower characteristics have always been considered of greater importance than the vegetative characteristics when the limits of the genus are defined. As flowers of *Dendrobium* have a certain visual similarity the plants have been placed into the one genus and the differences accommodated by the use of Sections. The validity of this is questionable but as there are an estimated 1000 species of *Dendrobium* very widely distributed, no taxonomist has yet been able to carry out a complete review of the genus as it stands today. Some have attempted in part, being limited to a given geographical area but it is the further comparison of plants between areas which is difficult to accomplish.

In some genera, e.g. *Phalaenopsis*, sub-sections are used to sub-divide the sections into smaller although significant groups having a narrower range of identifiable characteristics than provided by the Section.

Using *Dendrobium* as an example, the various sections accommodate such individual characteristics as—petals broadest near tip and twisted; or leaves overlapping and laterally compressed. Unlike many other families of plants the flower colour in Orchidaceae has little taxonomic value and if any significance is attached to it, the level of classification is lower than species. This may be referred to as a variety or form.

The term Sub-genus is sometimes used but differentiation between this term and a Section is not at all clear and depends on the taxonomist. Sometimes the term is used to describe a group of plants clearly belonging to a genus, but growing in isolation and differing slightly from the norm. It is not of great significance to the orchid grower but may be seen in various texts from time to time.

Further sub-division below the species is often used. There are in descending order, sub-species (subsp.), variety (var.) and form (f.), and must be used in that order only, e.g. it is incorrect to have a variety of a form but permissible to have a form of a variety.

These terms are strictly confined to species of orchids, i.e. those naturally occurring in the forest or bushland. The nomenclature and grouping of man-made hybrid plants is a different subject and is dealt with in a special chapter on hybrids.

Summary

The above may be summarised as follows:

		Endings
Class	Monocotyledon	
Family	Orchidaceae	-aceae
Sub-family	Orchidoideae	-oideae
Tribe	Vandeae	-eae
Sub-tribe	Sarcanthinae	-inae
Genus	*Phalaenopsis*	
Section	*Zebrinae*	
Sub-section	*Lueddemannianae*	
Species	*violacea*	
Variety	*bowringiana*	
Form	—	

The full name of the plant is *Phalaenopsis (Zebrina) violacea* var. *bowringiana*. Note that the generic name begins with a capital letter but the specific and varietal epithets begins with a small letter. The name of the Section is frequently omitted unless reference to it is important in the text. The words forming the name are to be written in italics but the abbreviation var. is not italicised.

3. PURCHASING PLANTS

One factor which frequently inhibits the purchase of an orchid is lack of knowledge about its needs and its flowers. To the stranger to orchid culture the name usually means nothing. Frequently the purchase is made because the plant is an Australian Native Orchid, therefore it must be easy to grow, a mistake made by many gardeners in respect of Australian native plants in general.

Australia is a big country having a wide climatic range from tropical to cool temperate, from wet to dry, from summer rains to winter rains. So the origin of the plant should be some guide to its cultural needs.

Specialised orchid nurseries are frequently helpful in advising on growing needs and flower type, as are members of an established Orchid Society. Outside of these one would be lucky to find anyone with even a modest and correct knowledge of the subject. This lack of guidance can ruin the perfectly good intentions of a purchaser commencing 'in orchids'. Early failures are disappointing and create the impression that the plants are difficult. Growing any type of plant can be difficult if it is completely new and no guidance is available.

In England during the 1800s orchid nurseries selling imported plants relied heavily on their collectors to supply guidance on growing conditions. Unfortunately these were either not accurate or misinterpreted and many orchids 'from the tropics' were baked to death in a hot dry house before tropical climate conditions became known.

The best first purchase for any person aspiring to orchid culture is a copy of the Australian Orchid Review (see Appendix 3). At this stage it is not the articles which are essential reading but the advertisements. Here we find the specialist orchid nurseries listed, many invite inspection or are willing to supply a catalogue of their wares.

Other chapters in this book suggest the type of plants you may like to grow; however, many beginners like to 'play the field' and quite rightly so, in order to get the feeling of growing orchids and how this appeals to them.

Do not purchase warm-growing orchids if you live in a cool climate unless you already have a heated glasshouse. Practically any orchid will grow well in the N.S.W. coastal climate in summer, if it is protected from hot N.W. winds. The winters, however, are too cold for warm growing orchids unless some heating is provided but this is a

graduated condition as micro-climates do exist and some plants are better than others at standing some degree of low temperature.

The term 'warm-growing' is used rather than 'tropical' as many orchids grow in the tropics at altitudes of 1500 metres or more and survive well in cool temperate climates. The other chapters in this book will allow some assessment of the catalogues to assist your choice.

In general beginners should not buy flasks of plants as raising the young seedlings or small plants is not simple. Many nurseries advertise *Cymbidium* mericlones as individual potted plants and these are a useful buy if your interest is in this genus. Mericlones usually come true to type and are good, otherwise the propagator would not have wasted time and money on producing these. Hybrid seedlings are much easier to produce but the buyer takes the risk that some plants may have worthwhile flowers and others very poor flowers. Seedlings of species are usually true representations of that species and may be purchased with every chance of obtaining good plants.

When obtaining plants from interstate nurseries, airfreight is by far the best method of transit. The cost of this should be pre-paid by the sender when placing the order. Those nurseries which deal mainly with mail orders state the minimum cost of air-freight in their listings and unless your order is large this will be sufficient to cover the transit cost. If the order is large some suppliers may even agree to pay the freight charges. It is also worth while adding $3 to cover home delivery costs by the airport courier. The usual transit time from door to door is within 24 hours for capital cities and major centres served by frequent airline schedules.

For near local or country nurseries one of the road courier services is the preferred method of transit if the nursery can arrange this. It provides a door to door service within 2 or 3 days.

Some nurseries will accept a bank-card number and charge your account accordingly. This is a very satisfactory method as the exact cost of the plants (you cannot always get those ordered) and freight can be charged so saving credit and under payment adjustments.

Another source of plants, often at very reasonable prices, is your local Orchid Society where surplus plants of members are auctioned at meetings. However, you get what you buy, with no redress and no guarantee of quality. Small pieces of a plant are not a good buy unless you have some expertise in culture, they take a long time to establish and may die during the process. Bid only for plants well rooted and not for pieces which have been poked into pots a month or so before auction. Not all plants need be in pots. A piece of bare rooted *Dendrobium*, for example, could well be tied to a piece of wood or cork and grown on.

Shows staged by orchid societies usually have a plant sales stall, plants coming from both members and nurseries. The prices are usually fair but bargains are unlikely. In general the plants are of good quality and this must be paid for and the quality plant will be more likely to survive than a debilitated plant.

Orchids are essentially slow growing plants hence are more expensive than the type of plant which can be grown from a cutting taken in March and sold as a flowering plant in October. Meristem culture has materially helped to reduce the cost of orchid plants. This largely overcomes the natural slow multiplication characteristics of the plant to produce new stems or offshoots.

Diseases of plants are dealt with elsewhere in this book but a word on spotting a diseased plant is really pertinent to the subject of purchasing.

Damaged leaves due to insects or fungi are often more of a nuisance than a problem as leaves are so persistent on orchid plants. The hole or damaged surface is there long after the insect has gone and black strips or spots on leaves due to fungal attack continue to be unsightly even though the fungus does not spread any further.

Any plants having shrivelled or collapsed pseudobulbs or stems should be regarded with suspicion although this does not necessarily indicate disease. The principal reason is a poor undeveloped root system. Either the plant is naturally a poor grower (happens at times with some hybrids) or has not been potted up long enough to develop a root system, or has been kept dry for some time.

However, if the pseudobulb or stem is squeezed and is soft or worse still a yellow-brown liquid exudes from it, the plant is diseased so avoid it.

Examine the underside of the leaves for scale insects or mites. A magnifier helps. Nursery stock is usually clean as they take definite steps to ensure that it is but stock from other sources cannot always be relied on. Scales are usually flat and brown and may be scraped off with the finger nail. In one form the males form a white cluster on the underside of the leaf. If present and you buy the plant, corrective action will be necessary as soon as possible.

Mealy bugs are another scourge. These live in the protected part of the leaf axils and are difficult to eradicate. They consist of a white flour-covered insect, quite small which sucks the plant sap.

As a general practice, quarantine all plants which come into your own area. Place them in an isolated place until they obviously have a good clean bill of health. This is generally indicated by new root and leaf growth (in the proper season). This practice also allows you to pull up and destroy any weeds which appear in the pots. There are some really bad weeds encountered which grow rapidly and seed just as quickly. If you ever let these loose in your collection you will spend a lot of time continuously weeding the pots.

It is also important that the first plants you buy should be well advanced and near to flowering size. This is a great spur to your ego when the plants flower and the rest of the family are impressed to see that your hobby is worth the money you are spending on it. With small plants this latter fact is not always apparent and can cause some deferment of your expected enjoyment.

However, this does not mean that you should buy valuable plants at first. Obtain plants which are likely to do well in your area, are easy to grow and will not damage your financial position and your status in the family if they perish due to your inexperience.

Descriptions of orchids and the housing of plants are dealt with in later chapters. Unless you live in a favourable area or restrict your interest to a small range of orchid plants, housing of some form is a must. So rather than spend up big at first, on plants, some of the available finance should be diverted to suitable housing.

It is appropriate to mention here that in N.S.W. and possibly in other States, native orchids are protected plants being in Group 3 and should only be grown for sale by a person holding a licence to do so. Persons who wish to pick plants, either from private land or from State forests must hold a Picker's Licence. The Licensee's personal identity tag must be attached to each bundle of Group 3 plants offered for sale. Applications for a Licence should be directed to the National Parks and Wildlife Service of your State.

4. HOUSING OF PLANTS

The housing necessary for orchid culture depends on three main factors:

1. The adaptability of the species you wish to grow to the prevailing climate.
2. The desirability of having the plants protected from rain, children, possums, insects and other forms of life.
3. The desire to keep plants within clearly defined boundaries.

Unless you are strictly a 'native to the area' grower the whole process of growing plants remote from their natural habitat is a compromise and necessitates some modification of the climate.

Firstly a word on climate. The two factors to consider are the temperature and humidity tolerance of the plants. Some indication of this is given in the chapter describing species. It does not necessarily follow that dwellers in the tropics have ideal conditions for all plants. For example, Singapore has a warm/hot climate with little variation in temperature yet many orchids are difficult to flower in such an environment. To overcome this the Singapore Botanic Gardens has a 'cool house' fitted with a refrigeration plant and sealed to keep the heat out rather than in as we in temperate climates need to do. Specimens of the temperate and high altitude orchids are grown, for at least part of their life, in this cool house. Other tropical countries, such as Indonesia, have established additional botanic gardens in their mountain regions so that the colder growing plants may thrive.

The temperature at your location can only be measured by a thermometer at your location and where you wish to grow orchids. The Weather Bureau measures temperatures in a box called a Stevenson Screen having a base height of about one metre above the ground. This may be located, for example, close to the sea, a lake or body of water, conditions quite different from those existing at your location. Unless you live next to the Weather Bureau it is advisable to measure the local temperature with a 0–50°C laboratory thermometer, not the domestic type. A laboratory thermometer is available for a few dollars from scientific and biological supply houses and will always be a useful tool for orchid culture.

Winter night temperatures are usually the minimum observed and should be measured at the height where the plants are to grow. Microclimates do exist. Tree canopies have a modifying influence on temperature, even the overhanging eaves of a house offer some protection from cold air and, of course, walls which have soaked up heat from the sun keep the temperature warmer at least for the first part of the night. Cold air flows downhill towards the lowest point and settles there. If the flow is trapped by a wall or fence that area is likely to frost up.

In general orchids can be divided into the following minimum temperature tolerances:

    4°C   10°C   13°C   15°C   17.5°C

If the temperature consistently falls below 4°C then some protection is needed. Those requiring 10°C can usually be grown in a 'cool glasshouse' in a mid temperature coastal climate while those needing higher minimum temperatures require a heated house in the same sort of climate.

Orchids tolerant of the minimum temperature which occurs at your location may be grown on tree trunks, dead tree stumps or on benches placed in the open under trees for some protection and shade in summer. This may mean *Vanda* in North Queensland or *Dendrobium speciosum* in Sydney.

Arboriculturists rather frown on the attachment of orchids to trees on the basis that they hold moisture against the bark and promote disease and insect penetration. Arboriculturists are interested in trees not in orchids so their viewpoint could be biased. The author has grown and seen others grow orchids on trees for years without any observable problem developing. This is the simplest form of housing for orchids. If this is done in dry country with low humidity it will be necessary to hose down during the day or place pans of water under benches to increase the humidity (see chapter on Substrates and Culture).

If some protection is required then a simple wooden structure using hardwood (75 mm × 50 mm) and shadecloth (28%) over sides and roof is ideal. The roof should be covered with clear corrugated fibreglass sheets to keep the rain off the plants, particularly the flowers. Most Councils seem willing to approve this type of structure.

The siting of the shadehouse is important to allow winter sun to penetrate. See Appendix 1 for data on sun angles, both vertical and azimuthal during the year. If a choice is possible select morning sun in preference to afternoon sun. In the morning the plants are cool, respiration rate is minimal and net photosynthesis is maximum. In the afternoon the respiration rate is higher due to mid-day temperatures and this minimises net photosynthesis.

If commencing in orchid culture site the shadehouse in the second best position. The best position should be reserved for the glasshouse to accommodate the less tolerant and more difficult to grow plants, a culture requiring more heating and more sunlight. A glasshouse enables the enthusiast to grow a wider range of plants.

Avoid laying a concrete floor for the shadehouse as this becomes covered with water and fertiliser solution and algae grows very nicely on this. In the author's experience the best type of floor, and it is very cheap, is one using a 5 cm thickness of road-base material usually available from suppliers of landscape or builders materials. It is black, so absorbs some heat from the sunlight and releases this at night. It is water absorbent so there are no puddles after watering but the humidity is maintained by evaporation of water stored in the road-base material. It can even be improved by a 5–7 cm layer of builders' sand underneath the road-base. Weeds may grow but the floor can be drenched with a weed killer without affecting the orchids. Cleanliness is important. Weeds tend to act as host plants for disease. Do not use black plastic sheet under the floor material as this does inhibit drainage.

If possible shield the house from cold winds and hot dry winds. The transit of wind past an enclosed structure takes heat from it, the heat loss in a 24 km/hour wind can be twice the loss in still air. Hot winds quickly dry out the plants, cause water deficiency within their tissues and generally raise the respiration rate to high levels.

As shadecloth comes in a width of 1.8 metres it is convenient and economical to use multiples of this. For example a house can be 2 × 1.8 m + 60 cm long = 4.2 m by 1.8 m wide. The extra 60 cm allows for a door of this width in the long side of the house. The height should not be less than 2.5 metres at the southern wall to allow for a near vertical panel of Weldmesh of 75 mm × 50 mm mesh, to hold plants on cork, tree fern or wooden blocks. A suggested house plan is shown in **Fig. 4-1** of this chapter. The southern wall may be fibro sheet (1800 mm × 900 mm) in lieu of shadecloth to deflect the wind which tends to knock over plants. If left unpainted or painted white, light will be reflected on to the plants hanging on the Weldmesh.

Benches are conveniently 60 cm wide and should preferably be made of Weldmesh cut (with bolt cutters) to size. A medium sized pair of bolt cutters is also a good investment for orchid growers and they cost very little for the labour they save. For small pots, 75 mm or smaller, use 75 mm × 25 mm mesh size. For larger pots the 75 mm × 50 mm mesh size is satisfactory. This can be laid on to a timber framework with cross members every 40 cm. Weldmesh has the great advantage of allowing good air circulation around the plants; essential for good growth and lessening the chance of fungal diseases.

The configuration shown in **Fig. 4-1** wastes very little space. The effective area for plants is 93% of the floor area which is exceedingly good. Many shadehouse layouts attain only 60% effective area for plants. The object with any design is to obtain maximum plant storage and minimum space for people.

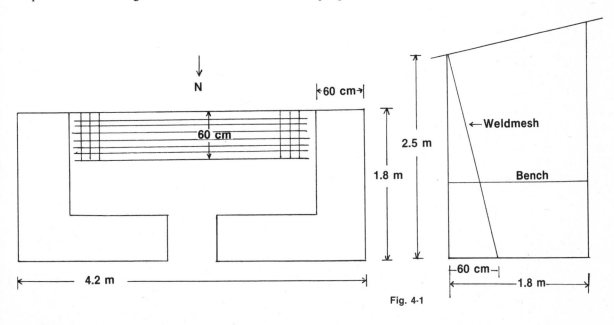

Fig. 4-1

Two tier benches are possible and have been receiving some attention recently. The lower bench is 60 cm from the floor, the upper one 138 cm high. Cool growing species liking shade can be grown on the lower bench, e.g. *Paphiopedilum* species. The high bench is useful for sun lovers. This approach increases very considerably the number of plants which can be housed. New fibreglass on the roof can cause the house to get quite hot on a sunny spring or summer's day. It may be necessary to nail some shadecloth (50%) to wooden battens and lay these loosely across the roof top in summer, removing these in autumn and winter. As the fibreglass ages it will discolour and provide extra shading. Unfortunately this shading is permanent and may ultimately make the house dark in winter and have to be replaced. Some new fibreglass material may be more resistant to decomposition but, in any case it is advisable to give a coat of an acrylic paint (clear) to the upper surface to lengthen the useful life of the material. It has been reported that old fibreglass may be rejuvenated by washing with a solution of tri-sodium phosphate (450 gms/4.5 litres), then brushing with steel wool to remove any loose fibres finally rinsing well with water.

Some growers like to use metal pipe as a framework, e.g. G.I. pipe and Downee clips and joints. Unless you have some skill in metal working the hardwood timber set into concrete in the ground to a depth of 30 cm, is ideal and long lasting. Additionally it is very easy to nail things to. If you are worried about termites a drench with Dieldrin (120 ml to 4.5 litres of water) around the posts will put a stop to these.

The next logical step from the shadehouse is to enclose the structure entirely in fibreglass sheeting or fit glazing bars to the walls (horizontally) and slide in sheets of horticultural glass (second grade cheap glass). The horizontal glazing bars (which can be obtained cut to the size you require) allow the glass to be slid along in the bars so providing 'open windows' for ventilation. A closed house needs a fan for ventilation in summer and additional shade over the roof. If you are tempted to fit a glass roof then a hail guard of chicken wire held about 30 cm away from the glass is essential. It also provides a very convenient structure over which to throw the extra shadecloth in summer. Do not submit to the temptation to 'paint' the glass outside with a white water soluble paint. A small house shadecloth will not break you financially and the painting is more trouble than it is worth. As warm air rises to the roof most of the heat escapes from the house through the roof. The heat which has been stored in the house from the sunlight can be kept in for longer by lining the house with an ultra-violet light inhibited plastic sheeting. A good material is Polyscrim LX which is 175 cm wide and is reinforced to avoid tearing. Some retailers of agricultural products will cut it to the length you require. This, of course, is more costly per metre than buying the full 50 metre roll. If the framework of the house is wood this allows the material to be secured with thin battens.

However, rather than enclose a shadehouse structure you may prefer to invest in a glasshouse. The purchase, construction and management of this type of housing is covered in Topic 1.

5. ANATOMY OF ORCHIDS

The purpose of this chapter is to illustrate and explain the various parts of the orchid plant. Those terms which are not covered in the first part of this chapter and are relevant to this book and orchid culture generally are listed in the Glossary on page 79. Explanations must necessarily be brief so only the major factors relative to culture are mentioned.

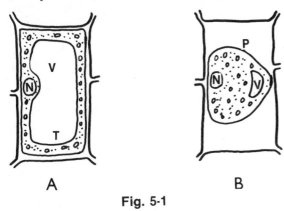

Fig. 5-1

The Cell. Fig. 5-1 illustrates at A, a typical plant cell having an outer wall of cellulose fibres crossed and interlaced. Inside this and pressed hard against it is the plasmalemma or cellular membrane. The diagram shows this spaced away from the wall only for ease of illustration. This membrane is formed from three layers and is a little less than 10 nanometres (Appendix 3) in total thickness, visible only under high magnification of an electron microscope.

The plasmalemma forms one boundary of the cytoplasm (shown stippled in **5-1A**) which contains the nucleus N and organelles. Prominent among these latter are chloroplasts in which much of the food manufacturing processes occur. The nucleus contains the chromosome material which determines the characteristic of the plant.

The inner boundary of the cytoplasm is another membrane—the Tonoplast marked T. Unlike animal cells, plant cells contain a vacuole, marked V, a large space full of water and water soluble substances, e.g. fertiliser salts. These are used by the cell as required. The presence of a high salt content in the vacuole encourages dilution from outside the cell and water enters through both membranes into the vacuole. This creates a turgor pressure which keeps the membranes taut and stretched and the plant looking healthy.

Fig. 5-1B shows a plasmolysed cell where the water has been withdrawn almost totally from the vacuole which has shrunken, the plasmalemma has come away from the cell wall and assumed a spherical shape. It is no longer stretched by turgor pressure of the vacuole. This condition has been caused by ex-osmosis, the salt concentration outside the cell (excess fertiliser residues) has pulled the water out of the cell. Recovery is possible if water is applied and the external salt concentration is reduced. Just as likely it may not recover and die. Therefore, it is particularly important that delicate root tissue should not be subject to high salt concentration and lack of water. Failure to keep the potting substrate moist can result in an increase in salt (fertiliser) concentration.

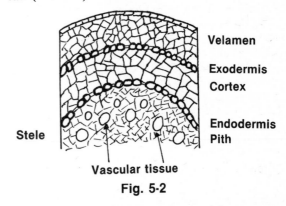

Fig. 5-2

The Root. Fig. 5-2 shows a partial transverse section of a root of an epiphytic orchid. The outside layers of cells, probably from 2 to 10, are dead cells and form the Velamen. This is a layer of water/air absorbing tissue over the inner part of the root and serves to collect water readily from the first rain (which contains nutrients washed from the leaves of trees, see Chapter 1) and pass these to the inner root. Also when full of air it insulates the root against water loss from within. In dry conditions the velamen cells, being devoid of cytoplasm, appear white which is said to be useful in reflecting heat away from the roots. In moist situations the velamen appears to be inhabited by Cyanobacteria (blue/green algae) but whether this is advantageous to the orchid, such as nitrogen fixation from the air, is not known and requires some investigation. When the root adheres to bark or other substrate the velamen does not form between the inner root and the substrate, being unnecessary.

Inside the root are two rings of thick walled cells called the exodermis (the outer) and endodermis (the inner). The exodermis in older roots becomes lignified or woody and gives some support to the root. Both rings of cells are provided with thin walled passage cells through which water and nutrients can pass into the centre of the root. Between the exodermis and endodermis is the cortex, 6 to 10 rows of living cells with thin walls, often used for the storage of starch grains as a food reserve.

Inside the endodermis is the stele (pronounced steel-ee) which houses the conducting tissue to transport water and nutrients upwards, by xylem tissue (pronounced zeye-lem) and phloem (flow-em) to conduct sugars and other substances to the roots. The xylem and phloem conducting tissues (vascular tissue) are arranged in bundles located just inside the endodermal ring.

The actual centre of the root inside the ring of vascular tissue is the pith, another set of cells used for the storage of starch. The number of vascular bundles varies from root to root but a large root of *Cattleya* may contain 20.

The tip of the epiphytic root in good health and growing well, should be green or green/purple for a distance of 2 cm. If this is not so then your growing conditions may leave something to be desired. A root having 'lumps' every cm or so along part of its length shows a stop/start type of growth, perhaps intervals of warmth interspersed with periods of cold; not good culture. Root health is most important in orchid growing and is a gauge of successful or poor culture.

Many geophytic orchids have a tuber (an underground stem) or the whole root is fleshy. In some cases the root is made up serially of thin and thick sections. These tubers or swellings are basically storage organs which survive dry seasons and bush fires and send up a new shoot next season. Many geophytes have twin tuberoid structures which the Greeks called 'orchis', meaning testicles, and from which the modern name 'orchid' is derived.

Growth pattern. Fig. 5-3. There are two major growth patterns in orchids. The first is called 'Sympodial' (5-3A) which has a wide variety of forms but is commonly the production of new stems (sometimes called pseudobulbs) from a creeping rhizome, roots arising from each new stem base (orhids do not have tap roots). *Cattleya* and *Bulbophyllum* are clear examples of this type of growth (see **Plate 6**) because of the normally long internodes, that is, the length of the rhizome between stems. Other orchids, such as *Dendrobium* frequently have very short internodes.

Fig. 5-3A

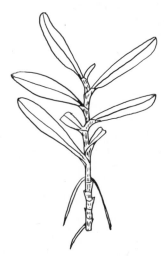

Fig. 5-3B

The second type of growth is 'Monopodial' (**Fig. 5-3B**) typified by the *Vanda* or *Ascocentrum* (**Plates 44 & 45**). As the name states it is of 'one foot' and the plant continues to grow upwards, sometimes young shoots are produced from the base (see Chapter 9).

In some orchids the stem is thickened usually for the purpose of water and food storage to enable the plant to survive dry periods. This thickened stem has become known as a pseudobulb or false bulb, but it is neither a bulb nor a tuber, but simply a stem and must be considered as such. Some long stems are referred to, for some mysterious reason as 'canes'. Why the word 'stem' is insufficient is not clear.

The Inflorescence. Fig. 5-4. The inflorescence may consist of a single flower as in some *Paphiopedilum* (**Plate 36**) or *Anguloa* or several flowers as in *Cymbidium* and *Vanda* (**Plate 43**) or many flowers as in some *Oncidium* (**Plate 26**).

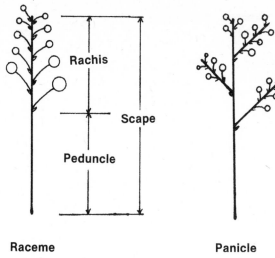

Raceme   Panicle

Fig. 5-4
Schematic diagrams of an inflorescence

The term commonly mis-applied to an inflorescence is 'spike'. Orchids do not have spikes unless there is some very obscure type of which the author is not aware. A *Gladiolus* has a spike where the sepals of the flowers are attached directly to the flower stalk, that is the flowers are themselves stalkless or sessile, having no pedicel. *Gladiolus* has a superior ovary, that is an ovary above the sepals and petals. Orchids have an inferior ovary below the flower so even a casual glance by a novice at an inflorescence shows that the flower is not sitting on the flower stalk. Although both ovary and pedicel are joined together they are distinct. The author dissected the ovary and pedicel of a very tiny flower of a *Schoenorchis*, which is rather obscure, and found that the ovary measured 2800 μ/m in length and the ovary plus pedicel was 6660 μ/m in length. This showed that the flowers did not form a spike but were attached by a flower stalk of 3860 μ/m or 3.86 mm. It is pleasing to see that some growers and Journal Editors are now using more appropriate expressions to describe the inflorescence rather than use 'spike'. The terms 'peduncle' and 'rachis' are often confused mainly due to misuse by speakers and authors and by failure to differentiate between the terms. The peduncle is the main stem that supports the inflorescence up to where the flowers are attached. The rachis is the upper part of the flower stalk from which the pedicels arise. The peduncle plus the rachis is called the scape. This latter term is often used for the flower stalk which terminates in a single flower, e.g. *Paphiopedilum*. The principal terms used in describing an inflorescence are raceme and panicle as shown in **Fig. 5-4**.

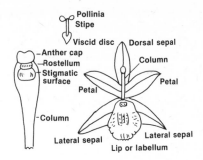

Fig. 5-5

The flower. Fig. 5-5. This diagram shows the simple and usual form of an orchid flower but many species have flowers where the parts are not immediately obvious. However, dissection of the smallest flower will show the same basic form. Some plants, e.g. *Bulbophyllum* have large sepals and very small petals (**Plate 6**) which appear as insignificant parts of the flower. Monocotyledons (see Chapter 2) typically have flower parts in threes, so the first whorl or ring of three parts is formed by the sepals, the next whorl by three petals of which the lip forms one. Instead of two further whorls of anthers as in other monocotyledons the stigma and anthers are formed into a column as shown in the diagram. It is typical of the orchid flower that there is some degree of union between the stigma and its supporting style, and the anthers and their supporting filaments. In most of our cultivated orchids the union is complete to form the column. In the Apostasioideae and Cypripedioideae (see Chapter 2) the union is not complete.

The top of the column is covered with an anther cap which may be lifted off gently with a toothpick to expose the pollinia (singular, pollinium). The diagram shows a 'pollinarium' consisting of two pollinia, the viscid or sticky disc and a stipe or stalk. There are many different types of pollinaria in the Orchidaceae and in this work it is only practical to describe and illustrate one of these. Because of its great variability the form of the pollinarium including number, shape and texture of the pollinia plays an important part in the classification of orchid plants. However, this must be used with some caution as there are a great many similarities between some genera, e.g. *Cattleya* and *Encyclia*. Even the number of pollinia is not consistent in the terms of our artificial generic classification, some departures from the expected norm are evident, e.g. whereas *Cattleya* has typically only four pollinia and *Laelia* eight pollinia, *Cattleya dormanniana* has four large and four small pollinia!

An interesting exercise with a pollinarium similar

to that illustrated, is to hold the sticky disc firmly and move the pollinia away from the top of the stipe. Note the elastic attachment thread called a caudicle which is non-cellular. The viscid disc and stipe are cellular and derived from column tissue. When counting pollinia be aware that some lots of four pollinia fit together snugly in pairs giving an apparent count of two. In others the two pollinia both have a distinct cleft which may lead to the belief that there are four pollinia. The cleft is only a cleft and there are only two pollinia. In some genera, e.g. *Dendrobium*, both viscid disc and stipe are absent, the four pollinia being in pairs but readily fall apart.

The Leaf. Fig. 5-6. The leaf shapes of orchids are many and varied as the coloured plates will show. Australia has some oddities from the twisted spiral type in *Thelymitra mathewsii* and *T. spiralis* in Victoria and Western Australia to *Dendrobium cucumerinum* which looks like a green mummified warty finger.

However, the importance of the leaf is in its food manufacturing ability (see Topic 4). The production of food depends on the entry of carbon dioxide into the leaf through the stoma (pl. stomata or as often used, stomates) which are breathing pores in the leaf surface.

Fig. 5-6, A, B and **C** show three pictures taken with a scanning electron microscope of these stomata. **Fig. 5-6A** is from a *Vanda* leaf magnified 1000 times, the small black square at the near bottom right of the photo is 20 μ/m across giving a stoma size in its maximum dimension of 10 μ/m, the size of a large soil bacterium. Disease causing bacteria are much smaller and can easily crowd through a stoma aperture. The cells around the aperture are guard cells which, by increasing and decreasing their osmotic pressure, close or open the stoma. **Fig. 5-6B** is from a *Dendrobium* leaf magnified 2000 times and showing a single stoma open. Note the wavy rills of wax covering the leaf surface which make it difficult for water (containing fertiliser) to spread over the epidermal cells and penetrate into the leaf unless some surfactant (detergent) is added to the fertiliser spray. The black marker in this photo is 10μ/m so the stoma aperture is 20μ/m here, twice as long as in *Vanda*.

Fig. 5-6C is from a *Phalaenopsis* leaf magnified 2000 times. Note the amount of apparent rubbish lying around looking like a rubbish tip. This is mostly waxy exudate from the epidermis. The black marker is again 10μ/m long so the stoma shown has a length of 15 μ/m. The size of stomata on a leaf is surprisingly consistent in size, shape and distribution.

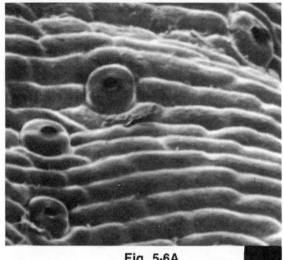

Fig. 5-6A

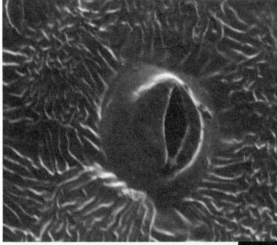

Fig. 5-6B

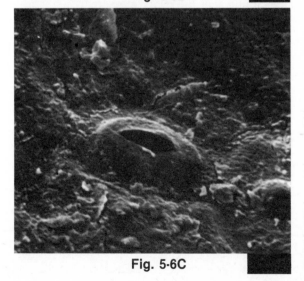

Fig. 5-6C

Ploidy. A term used to indicate the number of chromosomes in a nucleus. The chromosomes store the genetic information of the organism.

The normal somatic or body cells of the plant have two sets of chromosomes and are known as diploid, abbreviated as 2n. If during the process of mitosis (the multiplication of cells in the body) a separating membrane fails to form we then have twice the number of chromosomes in a cell, which becomes a 4n cell. If these 4n cells then multiply out the plant becomes known as a tetraploid.

The sex cells or gametes are formed from body cells by a process of meiosis, where the number of chromosomes is halved, so in a sex cell there are n chromosomes. This is necessary so that when sex cells from pollen merge with sex cells from the ovules n + n chromosomes again result in 2n chromosomes for the body cells. Sex cells from tetraploids have 4n/2 chromosomes or 2n. If a tetraploid is mated with a diploid, then 2n + n = 3n or a triploid results. Triploids usually grow well and often produce a large number of flowers hence are popular with growers of cut flowers. They are, however, not fertile or only slightly so, producing a few viable seeds instead of thousands.

There are other forms of ploidy, such as hexaploid or 6n chromosomes and aneuploidy where odd numbers of chromosomes are produced. Instead of 38 chromosomes (2n) a plant may have 35 or 41 chromosomes and be an aneuploid. The counting of chromosomes requires some experience, patience, many root or pollen squashes and equipment. A lot of work has been done on this subject and those interested could well refer to 'List of chromosome numbers in orchids' by Robert Duncan in *The Orchids* edited by Carl Withner, Ronald Press N.Y. 1959. Other listings have been produced from time to time.

As Genetics is a large subject of limited interest to growers it is not covered in this book. The above information is sufficient to allow newcomers to orchid culture to understand some of the terms used.

6. SUBSTRATES & CULTURE

There are perhaps, no two subjects which excite more discussion and argument among a group of orchid growers. Whatever they say, most are correct; which does not make the others incorrect. Although many growers tend to be very dogmatic about what is the best and only method of growing orchids the newcomer should try out various substrates and culture methods.

The most important thing to remember is that a plant responds to total environment made up from factors such as temperature, light, humidity, carbon dioxide, water and fertiliser. The experienced grower integrates all factors and adjusts each one for optimum results. Growing plants of any kind where they do not grow in nature is a compromise and he who provides the best compromise meets with greatest success.

The guide lines given in this Chapter are only starting points as a basis for further experimental work by you. Plants can accustom themselves to a given environment but any rapid change in this usually has a deleterious effect on them. For example, if a plant has been growing in mottled shade conditions, moving it to full sun in spring/summer is a rapid change. The plant should be placed in full sun in late autumn/winter to become more accustomed to high light intensity. With few exceptions, such as the so-called 'Jewel' Orchids and some of the mottled leaved *Paphiopedilum*, orchids are not grown for the appearance of their foliage and often the more 'beat-up' and degenerative the plant looks the better it will flower.

In their natural environment many orchids are stress tolerant plants coping with dry conditions, lack of adequate mineral nutrients or poor light. It is this stress tolerance which allows them to be grown under all sorts of conditions different from their natural environment. However, it should not be assumed as is often done by writers, that where an orchid is growing, is its optimum position and that growing conditions are perfect. As anyone who has collected orchids from the jungle knows quite well, the plants will most likely do better in the collector's glass-house than they ever did in nature.

Substrates

The substrate is whatever the plant is growing on or in. It may be the bark of a live tree, a piece of picket fence, a piece of cork or a pot full of bark, charcoal or other material. With very little exception the orchid plant needs a substrate which will not be sodden and which will allow good penetration of air. The prime example of this is a piece of hardwood to which the roots will cling; when doused with water the excess immediately runs off leaving the wood and roots to dry out. Various lesser types of drainage are used, for example, cork which is porous and retains some moisture for a while. A pot of bark pieces drains readily but moisture is retained in the pot for a longer period. A pot of charcoal will retain moisture for some time due to its porous nature. It also retains fertiliser but excess of this may readily be flushed out with water.

In nature orchids may be divided into two main groups when considering substrates.
1. Those which grow in the ground or appear to do so. These are geophytes.
2. Those which grow on trees (epiphytic) or on rocks (lithophytic). The latter usually send roots into the humus layer between the rocks or in cracks so they may even be considered as geophytes.
The distinction between the two groups is clear in some cases but there are shades of grey at times, even within the one genus, so some judgement is needed.

Substrates for Australian Native Geophytes
In this country we are fortunate in having, as native plants, many forms of geophytic orchids and the cultivation of these, after being neglected for a long period, is now becoming popular. This is probably due to the very active membership of the Australasian Native Orchid Society. The genera most frequently grown are *Pterostylis*, *Aciathus*, *Corybas*, *Caladenia* and *Diuris*.

For those who wish to pursue this culture the following substrate is recommended as a starting point. Use peat moss, sand and soil mixed in the ratio of 30:50:20. The high sand content will tend to open up the loamy soil but if this, itself, is quite sandy, adjust the mix accordingly. The addition of some fine gravel (a good substance to have on hand) perlite or small pieces of charcoal will also assist drainage. Good aeration of the root system with near drying out is essential. For a fertiliser use blood and bone (100 ml jar to 9 to 10 litres of substrate). Some potassium may be needed if the soils deficient in this mineral.

Substrate for Cymbidium hybrids
The beginner may most usefully and easily purchase a bag of Cymbidium compost marketed at garden centres and nurseries. This consists of a variety of substances including peat moss, rice hulls, charcoal, sand and soil varying according to the producer. Again good drainage is needed and the grower may add charcoal, gravel, perlite or broken crocks to suit his own needs.

Substrates for Epiphytes and Lithophytes
1. Live trees
The plant may be tied to a tree making sure that any good, live and firm roots are tied against the trunk. It is a common error to tie the plant securely to the tree and allow the roots to dangle. The roots should be tied in contact with the bark and not separated therefrom by a pad of sphagnum moss or similar. While this pad may keep the roots moist it prevents them from clinging to the bark. Plants may sometimes be secured into the fork of a tree, dead or alive, and then tied to the bark with a cloth or string tie. See also the chapter on 'Housing the Plants'.

2. Cork and hardwood
These are valuable for most epiphytes. *Dendrobium*, *Ascocentrum*, *Sarcochilus*, *Vanda*, *Trichoglottis* and many similar types of plants grow well on this form of substrate. Tie the plant to the cork slab or board but also ensure that the roots are in direct contact with the substrate as explained above. Cork comes in various grades and sizes. Pressed cork (available from cork merchants) is usually in slabs 90 × 30 × 2.5 cm and may be cut with a wood saw to size. Cork bricks (the size of a house brick) are also available and useful for those plants which creep around the substrate.

Some orchid nurseries have other forms of cork slabs available, usually of better quality and this is worth using. Fence pickets about 12 to 15 cm wide provide useful pieces of hardwood when cut to length. A piece of wire through one end of the wood or cork is a simple method of hanging the plants on the Weldmesh (see chapter on 'Housing the Plants').

3. Substrates in pots
Every gardener from long habit tends to try to force all orchid roots into pots, particularly if his experience in orchids is limited to hybrid *Cymbidium*. Although pots are convenient for transport most plants will tend to grow out of the pot and attach their roots to the wooden bench, framework or just remain in air. For small orchid plants needing rapid drying out of the roots (e.g. *Cattleya*) clay pots have a decided advantage. For larger plants clay pots are both expensive and heavy and not looked upon with favour by many growers.

The purpose of the substrate is to hold the plant upright (with the help of a stake), keep the roots confined for easy transport and provide a surface for the roots to cling to and grow on. In potted plants a stake should always be used until the plant becomes well established in the pot. Any wobbling of the plant severely damages the new root tips which die off to the detriment of future growth.

Pine bark, fir bark and charcoal are used in varying quantities by various growers. Other additives are marble chips (to give a slight alkalinity) perlite, vermiculite, broken clay pots and broken up polyurethane packing pieces. In fact, to the gardener, the potting material for epiphytic orchids looks like a load of rubbish, practically any inert or near inert material will do.

The choice of materials used in the pot will be governed to some extent by your proposed culture methods, so substrates and culture cannot be separated and treated as two independent matters. For example, if the interval between watering is to be long (relatively speaking) for your temperature, humidity and light conditions then the use of charcoal in the mixture has decided advantages. The bark used needs to be firm and hard; some pine bark is very soft and reduces very quickly to a soggy mess which will rot away roots.

4. Other substrates

There are other apparently geophytic orchids, *Paphiopedilum* being a good example, which grow, in nature in leaf mould on a calcareous soil or rock. A suitable substrate for these plants is a very open type mixture containing some of the following: bark, charcoal, sphagnum moss, perlite, leaf mould and dolomite. Some growers use marble chips in lieu of dolomite to open up the mixture and provide a small amount of calcium carbonate. When an orchid grows in rotting vegetation some humic acids are produced. The calcium carbonate, even in slight amounts tends to neutralise these acids.

Jewel orchids such as *Ludisia, Macodes* and *Goodyera* require a rich substrate very high in organic matter. In nature *Macodes petola* has been found growing in fine sand with an abundant supply of leaf mould.

In general it would be fair to state that the thinner the root the smaller the particles making up the substrate. For thick root *Vanda* for example one should use very large pieces of bark, charcoal or broken charts if this genus is to be pot grown.

Culture

In this chapter it is possible to consider culture in general terms only and leave more detailed comments for recording under the heading of particular species. However, the two are complementary and the general considerations are most important in enabling the grower to assess problems encountered.

For a plant to grow it must have energy and food materials to incorporate into its own structure. A plant can be fertilised heavily and often but without energy it will not grow. The ultimate source of all energy on earth is electromagnetic radiation from the sun. The most significant part of this, biologically speaking, is the part we can see, that is, visible light, electromagnetic radiation to which our own eyes respond and strangely enough the part to which plants also respond. Is there perhaps, some distant evolutionary reason for this? The electromagnetic spectrum is very wide, from gamma rays with a wavelength of less than 0.1 nanometre (refer Appendix 2) to radio waves measured in thousands of metres in length; yet the limited visible range is from 380 to 750 nanometres, and even less for some people. This very limited range is responsible for phototropism, photoperiodism and photosynthesis in plants.

The process of photosynthesis is mainly to trap energy from the sunlight and to activate enzymes within the cellular contents. This light energy shoots electrons away from the chlorophyll (a green coloured pigment, or that is the way we see it with our eyes) and by the time these electrons are restored once again to the chlorophyll this energy has become stored as chemical energy within the plant cell. It is this chemical energy, also available in the dark, that the plant uses to process the raw materials it receives into foodstuffs (for later use as an energy source) and into structural material like lignin and cellulose for stem and leaf and protein for life. The photosynthetic process applicable to orchids is treated in greater detail in Topic 4. For the present it is sufficient to say that photosynthesis is a building-up of energy and food in the plant. The opposite of photosynthesis is respiration. This is a process whereby foodstuffs in each plant cell are broken down to produce energy. It is often confused with breathing which is only a gaseous exchange process resulting from respiration and is not respiration itself.

It is obvious that if the build-up of energy and food from photosynthesis is not greater than the breakdown due to respiration the plant will not grow. It is the aim of good culture to see that the respiration rate is kept lower than the photosynthetic rate.

Factors which affect culture (apart from pests and diseases) are: Water; Relative Humidity; Radiation; Temperature; Fertilising and Air circulation.

These will be treated separately although in practice they all react together to produce a poor, an indifferent or a good plant.

Water

This is one of the most difficult factors to master as the water needs of each species may differ and it is also very dependent on the substrate and other environmental conditions, e.g. air circulation.

A few general rules may help.

(a) The higher the temperature (and light in some cases) the greater the water evaporation from the substrate, leaves and roots so the greater is the water demand. Conversely in cold weather very little water is needed by comparison.

(b) The thicker the stem, often called a pseudobulb, the less frequently watering need be done except in very hot weather. Some plants, e.g. *Phalaenopsis*, have no thickened stem and rely on limited water storage in the leaves, so frequent watering is needed.

(c) The greater the leaf area, particularly thin leaves, the greater the water supply needed.

(d) Ascertain the dormancy period of the plant and withhold water during this period.

The amount of water needed is affected by just about all factors such as Relative Humidity, Temperature, Light, size of leaf and so on. The opening and closing of the stomates in either light or darkness is also relevant to water needs. This latter subject is discussed in Topic 4.

Relative Humidity

This is expressed as a percentage of the water vapour held in the air at a given temperature compared to the amount which could be held under saturation conditions. If the amount of water vapour in the air remains constant the relative humidity will fall as the temperature increases.

For example:

Temperature =   21°C   R.H. = 65%

Temp. increases to   24°C   R.H. = 54%

Temp. decreases to   18°C   R.H. = 79%

The cells inside a leaf are bathed in water which evaporates and diffuses to the outside air via the stomates or leaf breathing pores. If the outside air has a high relative humidity, then the rate of this diffusion will be reduced and inhibited. As the evaporation of water cools the surface from which it was evaporated the leaf stays warmer, which is deleterious on a hot day. Additionally the transpiration stream is slowed down. This is the passage of water from the roots through the conducting tissue to the stem and leaf. As this water conducts the nutrients through the plant a reduction in the flow rate will reduce nutrient availability.

The humidity adjacent to the leaf will be greater than that read on a hygrometer in the house due to this constant evaporation of water. This build up of water vapour around the leaf reduces diffusion rate so it becomes important to circulate air, either by a fan or convection ventilation, around the leaf. Air circulation has other benefits which are stated later.

So to summarise, a low R.H. will increase the transpiration stream and nutrient conduction and cool the leaf. However, this has limits and will place the plant under water stress if the evaporation via the stomates is greater than the roots and conducting system can supply. This causes loss of turgor in the leaf which then appears to be flaccid and even slightly withered. If this is continued the withered leaves will not recover.

A very high R.H. decreases the transpiration stream and leaf cooling. Fortunately as the house temperature increases the R.H. falls which allows leaf cooling to continue.

Forced ventilation by a fan which pushes air out of the house keeps the R.H. around the leaf surface at a low level. A continuous high R.H. with no air movement promotes the establishment of fungal spores and consequent disease. The R.H. is a difficult factor to control; recommended levels are from 60% to 85% so a reasonable figure to aim for is 75% especially for lowland growing tropical plants. Evaporative coolers, misters, soaking the road-base floor with water; all help to keep up the humidity in the house.

Radiation

Visible light is just a small part of the radiation reaching earth from the sun. This radiation is divided into various sections depending on the wavelength of the radiation. Only three sections concern plantsmen, these being the ultra-violet, the visible and the infra-red parts of the spectrum. Appendix 2 should be consulted by those not familiar with some of the terms used here.

1. Ultra-violet radiation is short wave radiation from 10 nanometres to 380 nm and is not visible to the human eye. A nanometre is 10^{-9} metres or perhaps more familiarly one ten millionth part of a centimetre.

All wavelengths less than 295 nm are filtered out by the thin layer of ozone in the upper atmosphere; which is indeed fortunate because radiation at 254 nm not only kills micro-organisms (germicidal lamps) but most plants as well, if subject to this wavelength for a long period. This lethal effect is due to the action of this wavelength on DNA, the substance forming chromosomes with their associated genes. Plant breeders who wish to produce mutants might try exposing plants (perhaps young plants) to the radiation from a germicidal lamp. This radiation is harmful to the eyes so avoid looking at the radiating area of the lamp.

The intermediate wavelengths of UV radiation are from 280 to 315 nm. These are very photoactive causing sunburn and skin cancers in man. Plants absorb these wavelengths but by various means have minimised the likely harmful effects. The pigmentation of leaves by red/purple anthocyanins is very effective in screening out this harmful radiation. Some authors have previously regarded this pigmentation as a guard against high visible light, entirely ignoring the UV part. Some plants, when exposed to direct sunlight containing the UV radiation will develop purple pigments in the leaf cells.

The longer wavelengths of radiation in the UV spectrum from 315 to 380 nm have some effect on the plant reaction but it is difficult to separate this from the general response to visible radiation.

2. Visible radiation, commonly called light, has a waveband immediately above the UV. It is quoted variously as 400 to 700 nm and 380 to 750 nm and depends on the visual response of the individual human. The shorter wavelengths of 380 to 400 nm are seen as a purple-blue colour and the 700 to 750 nm wavelengths are seen as red and the so-called 'far red' colours. Other colours such as orange, yellow and green are due to excitation of the cones in the eye by intermediate wavelengths.

It is interesting to note that bees are red blind and do not respond to the longer wavelengths of the visible spectrum. They do, however, respond to some UV light and see an entirely different picture of the flower from that seen by humans as photographs taken with UV light show.

As chlorophyll absorbs light in both the blue (440 nm) and the red (660 nm), parts of the visible spectrum and reflects the intermediate wavelengths of 500 to 550 nm (green) the leaf appears to the human eye to be green.

If plants are grown under artificial light rich in 'red' and 'blue' but deficient in 'green' light the leaves appear dark in colour as there is insufficient 'green' light to reflect.

The exposure of leaves to bright sunshine often results in the degradation of chlorophyll so less 'green' light is reflected and the leaves appear yellowish. This is due to the carotenoid pigments in the 550 to 650 nm range which is yellow/orange.

In addition to photosynthesis, visible light is responsible for phototropism (bending towards the light) and photoperiodism (response to periods of light and dark for flower initiation).

3. Infra-red radiation as the name indicates, is beyond the red and is of wavelengths longer than 750 nm but not as long as radio/radar waves.

Infra-red radiation reaching the earth is limited to 750 to 2400 nm, the wavelengths longer than this being filtered out by water vapour and carbon dioxide in the atmosphere. The range from 750 to 1500 nm is largely reflected from plants. This is clearly shown by a picture of a plant community taken with IR sensitive film wherein all plant life shows up as a brilliant white. By contrast the usual black and white picture shows green plants to be relatively dark in colour.

Radiation is energy. It must be emphasised that all electromagnetic waves referred to in this section are a form of energy and as such can be converted to other forms of energy. The UV part of the spectrum has the greatest energy while the long wave infra-red has the least. This is one reason why the shorter wavelength UV radiations are dangerous to life. The bonds holding the molecules together and protein into its active shape are ruptured, so destroying life. Infra-red radiation has only sufficient energy to make molecules move a little more at a faster rate and this is felt as heat.

The major point of concern here is that this radiation energy can be converted to heat energy. This is made particularly evident in the so-called 'greenhouse effect' where some UV and lots of visible light pass through the glass. This energy is absorbed by walls, benches, the ground and plants and reradiated as heat energy in the infra-red part of the spectrum.

Sun-flecks
One never ceases to be amazed at the way plants respond to natural conditions. For example, leaves in natural communities have a constantly changing amount of illumination falling on them. Orchids growing in trees or even on the forest floor must also be subject to changing light intensities, that is sun-flecks, as the leaf canopy moves with the wind. Although no work has been done specifically with orchids, other plants have shown increased photosynthetic rate when subject to intermittent light at a periodicity of 6 to 7 seconds. A periodicity longer than this, say 1 minute, reduced the photo-synthetic rate. For many years it was (and perhaps still is) accepted practice in Sydney to grow *Cymbidium* plants outdoors in the mottled light of the 'gum

tree'. The rapid leaf movement in the wind provided short time periodicity of sun-flecks so perhaps a cultural method found by experience is confirmed by experiment. Much more work needs to be done on the subject of light before its full affect on plant culture is realised.

Light measurement

One constantly reads in various orchid journals that a certain species or genus requires so many foot-candles of light or so many lux (10.67 lux = 1 ft. candle). This can be measured with an incident light meter or sometimes a conversion table is given so that reflecting light meters (photographic) can be used to estimate the incident light intensity. Light meters have a response which is maximised at the centre of the visible spectrum about 550 nm or 'green' and fall off very much in response at 440 nm and 660 nm. This is very similar to the colour acuity of the human eye but plants respond to the visible spectrum in quite different ways to the human eye. For example, 'green' is near useless light to the plant whereas the blue and red of 440 nm and 660 nm is valuable. This method of measurement is of little value unless it is used for comparison between two growing sites and even then one has to be careful that any material interposed between the light source and the meter is not affecting the mid spectrum, i.e. green, which will cause wide differences in meter reading.

Although this method of measurement has its limitations it is currently the simplest to use. Radiant energy falling upon a surface is measured in watts per square centimetre or calories per square centimetre. One calorie per sq. cm. is called a Langley and the reader may see reference to this unit in literature dealing with sunlight and climate. The measurement of radiant energy is not simple and is unlikely to displace the foot-candle from popular literature for some time.

Temperature

All biological systems are temperature dependent. Those which depend on enzyme reactions are noticeably more dependent than those which are essentially physical. A plant can do little to control its temperature and is largely dependent on ambient conditions. This has contributed to a wide geographical distribution of plant life; those which will grow only in warm climates and those which thrive in alpine conditions being two extremes. Although orchids are rather adaptable plants they still have their limits. Many will not flower in consistently warm climates; others will pass out in consistently cool conditions; others refuse to grow if it is too hot or too cold. For optimum results it is necessary to govern temperature or to position plants where the desired temperature range is available.

Both photosynthesis (the build up of tissue, food reserves and energy) and respiration (the degradation of food reserves to supply energy) are enzyme controlled processes and are therefore very temperature dependent. Between 5 and 15°C there should be a rapid rise in activity with an optimum value somewhere between 20 and 30°C declining above this value. The exception to this are C_4 plants which are essentially tropical, utilising high light intensities and high temperatures having an optimum temperature around 35 to 40°C. The common example is sugar cane and only two orchids are so far known to exhibit this highly specialised leaf anatomy, viz. *Arachnis* cv Maggie Oie (**Plate 1**) and *Arundina graminifolia* (**Plate 2**) (Avadhani & Arditti, 1981). Other orchid plants appear to have an optimum high temperature of about 25°C.

For many orchids flowering is induced by a low temperature and it is recommended that the night time temperature should be 5 to 10°C lower than the daytime reading. It has been reported that growers in tropical and sub-tropical climates can induce flowering of some types of orchids, which would not otherwise flower in such high temperatures, by throwing a bucket of cold water (10°C) over the plants for a few nights. Like much information of this type it is not supported by proper experimental and scientific evidence and is given here in the hope that some researcher will come up with some quantitative data on the subject.

Keeping temperature down to optimum values is just as important to good culture as keeping the temperature above the minimum for growth. The most popular method of cooling the house, other than just ventilating it, is to use the evaporation of water. The device to do this is the evaporative cooler, where water drips or runs over a wad of mesh through which air is blown by a fan. At 20°C one gram of water converted to water vapour requires 2428 Joules (580 calories). By this forced evaporation of water the air is cooled and blown into the house. It is inferred that heated air is blown out at the same time. This method also increases the amount of water vapour in the house, which on a hot day may well be desirable to maintain the relative humidity. However, one point about this is often overlooked, the moisture laden air will be heated and as a result will be able to hold more moisture, but there is a limit to this. If the R.H. reaches 100% the water vapour will condense out of the air and give back the 2428 Joules (580 calories) to the surface upon which it condenses. Therefore, to ensure continued cooling the moisture laden hot air should be exhausted from the house.

If man-power is no problem an enclosed house may be cooled by damping down frequently during a hot day using a fan to exhaust the air. A misting jet, switched on and off automatically, placed in front of a fan is also a useful air cooling method. All of these depend on the latent heat of vapourisation of water to extract heat from the air.

Sometimes hot winds cause an ambient temperature of 35 to 40°C, so even shadehouses need cooling. Ventilation, natural or forced, will not reduce the temperature below ambient so the evaporation of water may be needed at times for shadehouses, particularly those with some form of solid roof material.

Ventilation

Many small glasshouses are fitted with some moveable panels called ventilators but on their own these are grossly inadequate. To cool a house, even in a mild sunny climate, requires about 20% to 50% of the roof to open up. This is clearly not a proposition for a glasshouse or even a roofed shadehouse. To secure adequate air movement in summer a fan is needed unless one lives in the mountains with very mild temperatures in summer. This fan is usually better if it is the blow-in type rather than suck-out and needs to move an amount of air equivalent to the glasshouse volume every minute. Some of the larger commercial houses use many fans with blades 120 cm diameter in order to move enough air.

This air movement is not only needed for cooling but to renew the depleted carbon dioxide necessary for plant growth. The carbon dioxide concentration in air is around 340 parts per million. Around the leaf surface this concentration is very much reduced due to the continued absorption of this from the air so creating a smaller diffusion gradient. The air needs to be forcibly displaced with fresh air to restore the amount of CO_2 around the leaf surface. Many growers are content to see the more mobile parts of their plants nodding gently in the moving air. This indicates to them that sufficient renewal of CO_2 is occurring.

Many plants, including a lot of orchids, open their stomates or breathing pores shortly after sunrise and close them shortly after dark when the internal CO_2 concentration builds up as photosynthesis (hence the using up of the CO_2) ceases. This means good air circulation just after sunrise is needed. However, many other orchids, particularly those epiphytes of the tropics act in the reverse manner. Their stomates are closed during the day to conserve water which can be in short supply in a windy tree top. When darkness falls, the temperature drops and the need for water conservation lessens, the stomates open and CO_2 is absorbed by the plant and stored as an acid in the cells. In this case it is obvious that ventilation is needed at night which is easy enough in summer but rather difficult in winter when the house is closed up to conserve heat.

This latter type of plant, often called a CAM plant, short for Crassulacean Acid Metabolism, is represented by many thick leaved tropical plants including *Vanda*, *Aerides*, *Angraecum*, *Cattleya*, *Laelia* and others. Not all species of these genera are CAM and also species of other genera have been found to have a CAM response (see Topic 4).

Shadehouse growing of CAM plants presents no difficulty in this respect providing the night temperatures are sufficiently high.

Fertilising

Each grower has his own favourite methods developed over a period of time and which he regards as unquestionably the best. Only two recommendations will be made here:

1. Use a little fertiliser at a time. Orchids are not gross feeders and the rate shown on the packet can well be divided by 2 or 4. In nature, orchids growing on trees must rely on rain, which can carry quite a lot of nutrient, some exudates from the leaves of the host tree and the decomposition of bark, mosses, leaves and so on, all of which add up to a small amount delivered often. Try to copy this method.

2. Avoid the use of solid fertiliser salts in pots growing epiphytic orchids.

7. THE NAMING OF HYBRIDS

What is a hybrid? It may be defined as an organism which is the offspring of a union between two different races, species or genera.

So a union between the pollen gametes and the egg gametes (a gamete is a sex cell) of two different species is a hybrid. A plant derived from two species is called primary hybrid and these, if fertile, may then be used to create further hybrids and so on and so on.

Although plant breeding by man is a very old art, the hybridisation of orchids is comparatively recent. The delay was due to lack of understanding of the structure of the orchid flower, as the column containing the pollen and stigma is rather different from most other plants. In the light of our present knowledge this reason is difficult to comprehend but both botanists and horticulturists were not so plentiful in the 1800s as they are today.

William Herbert reported in 1847 that he hybridised (or crossed) orchid plants and obtained a seed case (a capsule). These seeds were not grown to maturity. A similar attempt in 1849 by another English gardener named Robert Gallier was also unsuccessful; the seedlings died.

The first orchid hybrid to be grown and flowered, in 1856, was a plant called *Calanthe* × Dominii, the work being done by John Dominy who produced 25 hybrids before his retirement in 1880. (These days retirement is no barrier to the production of hybrids!)

Fortunately for orchid fanciers various publications over the years have kept track of hybrid plants, the most comprehensive and modern publication is Sanders' *Complete List of Orchid Hybrids*. See Appendix 3.

Naturally only those hybrids which are registered have any standing among hybrid enthusiasts and the commercial orchid growers. There must be many thousands of hybrids produced where the owner did not bother to register these or the plants were not worth the effort of so doing. Not all hybridisers or owners are enthusiastic about registering the result of their handiwork and are content to exhibit their plants at local shows. Registration is left to commercial organisations or to dedicated hybridists as reference to *'The Orchid Review'* centre pull-out will show. This monthly journal lists new orchid hybrids registered during a stated month and is a most useful and up-to-date reference for those interested in this area of orchidology. The American Orchid Society Bulletin also lists new hybrids. See Appendix 3.

Just a brief word on the registration of hybrids of any type. The International Society of Horticultural Science based in The Hague has established several Commissions each dealing with some facet of horticulture. One such Commission is for Nomenclature and Registration. This Commission then appoints various International Registration Authorities for the hybrids of various plant genera. The International Registration Authority for orchids is the Royal Horticultural Society, Vincent Sq. London SW 1P 2PE.

The naming of plants is governed by two International Codes, the first being for Botanical Nomenclature, the second being for 'Cultivated Plants' which includes hybrids. This latter publication is the responsibility of the International Commission for the Nomenclature of Cultivated Plants. However, the naming of hybrid orchids has special problems made more difficult by the extreme promiscuity of orchids generally where not only different species interbreed but also many genera interbreed readily. To provide an authoritative reference to the problems of orchid hybrid nomenclature the International Orchid Commission has produced a handbook on the subject, see Appendix 3. As with any set of Rules the expression of these must be done carefully and often with much wordiness. Many people may find interpretation difficult or even unnecessary to the full extent, having only a passing interest in the technicalities of the subject. To facilitate the understanding of these Rules some guidelines on the major points are given here, in a very un-rule like language and this may be all many growers wish to know about the subject.

The naming of species was mentioned in Chapter 2 The Orchid Family. Briefly, to recapitulate, an orchid species must have at least two words to its name. The first term is the generic name, familiar as *Cymbidium*, *Cattleya*, *Dendrobium* and so on. The second word is the specific epithet (not a name) which indicates the species within the genus. The two words together constitute the specific name, e.g. *Cymbidium dayanum*; *Cattleya bowringiana*; *Dendrobium kingianum*. Notice that the generic name and specific epithet are in italics when printed, or underlined, if in type. As explained in an earlier chapter the use of specific epithet on its own is improper, careless and sloppy.

Sometimes a third word is used to indicate a variety. It is called a varietal epithet and when added to the specific name all three terms become the varietal name, e.g. *Cymbidium lowianum* var. *concolor*, the abbreviation var. not being in italics.

Varietal names can be applied only to species found in the wild and refer to a population of plants having some characteristics different from the species type. A varietal name is generally given to a population by a botanist, not an orchid grower. In this respect it is most important to differentiate between varietal epithel and a cultivar epithet. Many orchid growers and exhibitors are grossly ignorant of this point and one constantly sees, at shows, a hybrid referred to as a certain variety. Only a species may be a variety.

If a grower has cultivated one plant (and the 'one plant' is emphasised) of a species (whether collected from the bush or jungle or raised from seed by him or someone else) the plant may be given a cultivar epithet which is a fancy name (not in Latin form). This cultivar epithet is enclosed within single quotation marks, e.g. 'Londoner'. This epithet is selected and given to the plant by the owner but more on the difficulties of this later. Not many species have been given cultivar epithets but occasionally a grower who has an outstanding single plant, (a clone) may wish to further identify it, particularly if it has won a prize on a show bench. If a species is given a cultivar epithet, then the name of the plant consists of three words, or four if it is applied to a variety of a species, e.g. *Cymbidium simonsianum* 'Planting Fields', which won an award, a Certificate of Cultural Merit. Cultivar epithets may also be applied to hybrids but cultivar epithets are not registered by the I.R.A. for orchids, whereas such are registered by Authorities for some other plant genera. Orchids are such prolific producers of seed that hundreds or even thousands of plants can often be produced from the fertility of one cross or hybridisation. Even if 10% of these are any good and worthy of a cultivar epithet, the thousands of plants and the hundreds of hybridisers would make registration of these a nightmare.

So what name is registered by the I.R.A.? The method used to show the parentage of a hybrid is called a formula. An example of this is

Cattleya bowringiana × *Cattleya elongata*

and this is the formula used whenever these two species are hybridised anywhere in the world and by anyone at all and irrespective of which is the pollen parent and which is the seed parent.

Orchidologists have used fancy names to describe such a cross-breed for many years but in a manner which was contrary to the rules of nomenclature and to the breeders of all other plants. The solu-

tion to the problem was resolved at a meeting between Dr W.T. Stearn and David Sander, where it was agreed that the multitude of plants produced by orchid hybridists should be called a Grex, meaning a swarm or flock. The adoption of this system then allowed the addition of a cultivar epithet in the same manner as used by other horticulturists. 'Orchidologists had come back into the nomenclatural fold' (W.T. Stearn in Two Thousand Years of Orchidology, 3rd World Orchid Conference, London 1960).

The hybrid formula given above has now been given the grex epithet of Elbowri (a fancy name, capitalised but not in quotation marks and not italicised) so the plant is now called *Cattleya* Elbowri but without an up-to-date hybrid listing one would not know this, whereas the formula gives a clear indication of the parentage and may be preferred by some growers. It is not incorrect to use the formula as some may think; it is a matter of preference.

Two hybrid plants may be interbred, e.g. *Oncidium* Susan Perreira × *Oncidium* Persian Red. Note that the generic name is still in italics (or underlined) but the grex epithet is a fancy name as before. This hybrid has now been registered as *Oncidium* Fire Opal.

Someone with an outstanding clone of this plant, after it has flowered, may wish to add a cultivar epithet and call this one plant *Oncidium* Fire Opal 'Goldilocks'. All offshoots, subdivisions, back bulbs and the like of this one plant can be known by this name.

Perhaps a species may be bred with a grex, e.g. *Oncidium* Pert × *Oncidium henekenii*. This has been registered as *Oncidium* Wild Honey. It must be becoming more difficult to think up grex names as the years go by.

So far this system has not presented any great problem but many genera of orchids also interbreed. Dominy, mentioned earlier in this chapter, and his successor, John Seden had, by 1905, raised 500 hybrids including some intergeneric hybrids. How should these be named? The answer was given by the naming of cross breeding of two non-orchid genera *Lapageria* and *Philesia*. The hybrid was given the generic name of *Philageria*. So an intergeneric hybrid between *Laelia* and *Cattleya* became *Laeliocattleya*.

A few examples are listed below:
Epiphronitis is *Epidendrum* × *Sophronitis*
Brassidium is *Brassia* × *Oncidium*
Ansidium is *Ansellia* × *Cymbidium*
Arachnoglottis is *Arachnis* × *Trichoglottis*
However this simplification did not last for long. With four genera contributing to the hybrid a

generic name like *Brassosophrolaeliacattleya* for a hybrid with parents in the genera *Brassovola*, *Sophronitis*, *Laelia* and *Cattleya* was just too much to say and write on a label. The difficulty was solved in 1950 at the Stockholm Botanical Congress when words ending in -ara were used, e.g. *Potinara* for the four intergeneric cross given above. This becomes a true generic name and the plant must be listed under this name.

A new generic name formed for three or more generic parents is derived often from the name of an eminent orchidologist and terminated in -ara, e.g. Yamadara, Vaughnara, Wilkinsara, Wilsonara, Kawanishiara and many others.

Hawaiiara Surprise is a hybrid between *Renopsis* Embers and *Vanda stangeana*; (*Renopsis* being a bigeneric hybrid between *Renanthera* and *Vandopsis*).

It is incorrect to use a grex name which has not been registered. Any hybrid of stated parentage can have only one grex name and one task of the I.R.A. is to prevent duplication of grex names and the allocation of another grex name to a parentage already registered. However, once registered, the name becomes the property of the world. Any hybrids resulting from a cross between the stated parents, whenever and wherever made, are known by this grex epithet. This may sound peculiar to many plant hybridists but any other method would result in hopeless confusion.

Whereas the allocation and use of grex epithets is reasonably well controlled, the use of cultivar epithets is wide open and uncontrolled except in a gentlemanly way. If you had a plant of say, *Dendrobium kingianum* which won an award and was considered by many as an outstanding plant you could select and apply a cultivar epithet. You may select 'Sydney Town' so the plant would be known as *Dendrobium kingianum* 'Sydney Town', but before selecting such a cultivar epithet you would be morally obliged to seek advice whether this name had been used before. Furthermore you should arrange for some recognised orchid journal to publish this cultivar epithet perhaps with a plant description and photograph. This at least informs others in future that you have some claim to this epithet. Unless this is done others cannot be expected to acknowledge your prior claim. If this plant is subsequently divided up and sold or given away the recipients should continue to use this cultivar epithet and of course, pass this on with future divisions of the plant.

The treatment of this subject here is not exhaustive but should be sufficient for the uninitiated to see through the gloom and mystery that apparently surrounds orchid hybrid naming. In point of fact it is clear although quite complex and is only confused terribly by growers who seemingly try not to follow the system or are ignorant of it.

While the Rules and proposals in the Handbook on Orchid Nomenclature and Registration may have some deficiencies and shortcomings at least they lay down a system which, if followed by everyone concerned, ensures some consistency in the naming of hybrids.

1. *Arachnis* Maggie Oei

2. *Arundina graminifolia*

3. *Amesiella philippinensis*

4. *Angraecum eburneum* var. *giryamae*

5. *Brassia verrucosa*

6. *Bulbophyllum dearei*

7. *Cattleya* hybrids

8. *Cattleya amethystoglossa*

9. *Cymbidium suave*

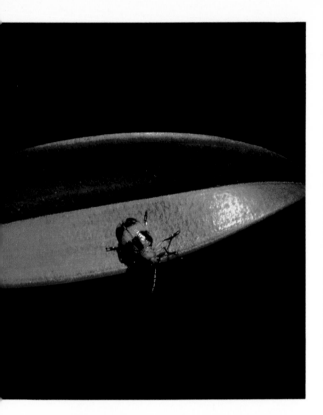

10. Dendrobium Beetle

11. *Coelogyne flaccida*

12. *Cymbidium* miniature

13. *Coelogyne massangeana*

14. *Dendrobium discolor*

15. *Dendrobium concavissimum*

16. *Dendrobium anosmum*

17. *Dendrobium spectabile*

18. *Dendrobium sanderae*

19. *Dendrobium thyrsiflorum*

20. *Dendrobium thyrsiflorum*

21. *Dendrobium falcorostrum*

22. *Dendrobium linguiforme*

23. *Dendrobium tetragonum* var. *giganteum*

24. *Dendrobium aemulum*

25. *Oncidium flexuosum*

26. *Oncidium flexuosum*

27. *Ludisia discolor* var. *dawsoniana*

28. Orchid Fruits

29. *Phalaenopsis lueddemanniana*

30. *Phalaenopsis*

31. *Phalaenopsis violacea*

32. *Phalaenopsis schilleriana*

33. *Phalaenopsis stuartiana*

34. *Paphiopedilum parishii*

35. *Paphiopedilum argus*

36. *Paphiopedilum callosum*

37. *Paphiopedilum insigne*

38. *Renanthera monachica*

39. *Rhynchostylis gigantea*

40. *Trichoglottis philippinensis* var. *brachiata*

41. *Vandanthe rothschildiana*

42. *Vanda* Wongsi × *Ascocenda* Meda Arnold

43. *Vanda tricolor* var. *suavis*

44. *Vanda hindsii*

45. *Vanda stangeana*

46. Nursery Bangkok

47. Native plants at orchid show

48. Corner of author's glasshouse

8. DESCRIPTION OF PLANTS

The photographs in the coloured plates have been selected, in the main, because they illustrate some point made in the text and not for their photographic excellence. In the descriptions which follow those marked with an asterisk (*) are ideal for those commencing to grow orchids. The newcomer is frequently confused by names and whether any particular orchid is easy or difficult to grow or requires special conditions.

Most of those illustrated are species. Hybrids come and hybrids go but species go on for ever. While species are usually a little more difficult to grow than hybrids a knowledge of the former is a valuable background to further orchid culture.

Growing conditions can only be given in broad terms for even in the Greater Sydney area the climatic differences are quite significant and a warm glasshouse in one location may be replaced by a protected area in another.

Plate 1. *Arachnis* Maggie Oei (Maggie wee)
Tribe Vandeae, Sub-tribe Sarcanthinae.
This is a typical tropical orchid cultivated as a cut flower in Singapore where it flowers continuously in open fields. A hybrid between *Arachnis flos-aeris* and *A. hookeriana* var. *luteola*. It may grow well enough in a glasshouse in temperate regions but could well be difficult to flower.

Plate 2. *Arundina graminifolia*
Tribe Arethuseae, Sub-tribe Bletiinae.
This is the 'weed' orchid referred to in the text as growing wild on the hillsides of Malaysia.

Plate 3. *Amesiella philippinensis*
Tribe Vandeae, Sub-tribe Sarcanthinae.
This plant is often erroneously referred to as *Angraecum philippinense*. The genus *Amesiella* was created by Schlecter and published in 1926 just after his death. Garay formally published the description of the species in 1972. A beautiful miniature found in the mountainous regions of Luzon and Mindoro at 750 metres. Requires heated house in cool temperature climate.

Plate 4. *Angraecum eburneum* var. *giryamae*
Tribe Vandeae, Sub-tribe Angraecinae.
This is a very large fast growing orchid the flower having a long spur which needs the long probiscus of a moth to reach the nectar. It is an example of the rewarding of quite specific insect pollinators mentioned in Chapter 1. The leaves are some 30 to 50 cm long and 5 cm wide, large and leathery. It needs plenty of light to flower but will do so prolifically in the Sydney climate if given heat in winter.

Plate 5. *Brassia verrucosa**
Tribe Epidendroideae, Sub-tribe Oncidiinae.
This plant is sometimes known as *B. brachiata* a name given by Lindley in 1842 but the name *B. verrucosa* precedes this by two years so is the valid name. This should be in every collection. It flowers in Sydney in November–December and develops rapidly into a specimen plant for a 30 cm pot. It is very easy to grow and will withstand temperate winters with only slight protection against frost and cold air. It is a native of Central America, Costa Rica and Mexico.

Another easily grown plant of the same genus is *B. gireoudiana**. Both species are readily available.

Plate 6. *Bulbophyllum dearei*
Tribe Epidendreae, Sub-tribe Bulbophyllinae.
Perhaps this does not have a great appeal to many, being an orchid for the specialist. It flowers in Sydney in October and is a native of Borneo and believed to require heat in winter. The illustration shows the use of compressed cork 25 mm thick as a substrate for epiphytes.

Plate 7. *Cattleya* hybrids
The large flowered type shown here is typical of the many available. Generally these require about 13°C minimum temperature in winter.

Plate 8. *Cattleya amethystoglossa**
Tribe Epidendreae, Sub-tribe Laeliinae.
This is a beautiful plant, very easy to grow in temperate climates without much protection. It is a native of Brazil and flowers about mid-summer. Readily available and really one worth growing.

Plate 9. *Cymbidium suave**
Tribe Cymbidieae, Sub-tribe Cyrtopodiinae.
An Australian native orchid to be found growing in the bushland even around Sydney. It is a protected plant (as are *all* orchids) but is available from orchid nurseries or from divisions by private growers. The plant shown is growing outdoors in the author's garden where it remains all year. It is planted in a hollow log which is typical of its normal habitat. In the bush the orchid tends to send its roots for long distances along cavities in tree trunks and branches. Its decline after years of cultivation is often attributed to lack of root run.

Plate 10. Dendrobium Beetle
A pest of orchids, but principally a pest of *Dendrobium* where this is grown.

Plate 11. *Coelogyne flaccida**
Tribe Coelogyneae, Sub-tribe Coelogyninae.
The inflorescence is pendant in this species from Nepal, Sikkim and Burma. It is very easy to grow into a large pot plant with several racemes in flower simultaneously.

Plate 12. This is a typical miniature hybrid *Cymbidium** which has become enormously popular with Australian growers because of the small amount of space taken up compared with the large type hybrids. These mini plants flower prolifically as seen by the illustration. They grow well outdoors under trees.

Plate 13. *Coelogyne massangeana**
This is another species and comes from the mountain areas of Java, Sumatra and Malaysia. It is a good example of a tropical orchid which grows well in temperate climates without heat in winter. In cold areas some protection may be needed. Widely grown and easy to obtain, for every collection.

Plate 14. *Dendrobium discolor*
Tribe Epidendreae, Sub-tribe Dendrobiinae.
This is a very robust grower from Australia and New Guinea with stems up to 120 cm or more in height in culture, larger in its natural habitat. Several racemes 60 cm in length rise from the upper part of the stem so the plant requires considerable space. It is a member of the Section Ceratobium (from Ceratos— a horn) and is often called the antelope *Dendrobium* because

of twisted petals. The flowers are large, typically 50 mm in diameter, golden brown in colour but some variation is possible. It is principally a lowland plant in Australia, growing from Tropic of Capricorn to Cape York peninsula. Very worthy of cultivation but does need heat in southern climates.

Plate 15. *Dendrobium concavissimum**
This is a New Guinea species common at 1500 metres in humid situations. The flowers appear in clusters on the leafless stems around October. Although essentially tropical its natural altitude indicates that it is satisfactory in a modestly warm climate. This plant is typical of many tropical *Dendrobium* species in producing flowers on what appears to be a dead stem. Hence such stems should never be removed from the plant until they are yellow and withered.

Plate 16. *Dendrobium anosmum*
A plant of the Section Eugenanthe which includes some of the largest flowered species of the genus. This species occurs in the Philippines where it is fairly common, through to Sumatra and New Guinea. It grows in lowland rain forest so requires warm conditions in a temperate climate. This species was named *D. macrophyllum* by Lindley in 1839 but this name refers to another *Dendrobium* so cannot be used. In 1861 the name was then changed to *D. superbum* but this allocation was preceded in 1845 by Lindley who gave the plant its name *D. anosmum* which is correct today. There is also a variety from the Philippines with very much longer stems and fragrant flowers which is called *D. anosmum* var. *superbum* so some care is needed when naming this plant. The New Guinea species has paler sepals and petals with a white margin around the lip.

Plate 17. *Dendrobium spectabile*
This species is native to New Guinea and the Solomon Islands but is cultivated widely in the tropics. The stems grow from 60 to 120 cm with flowers 7 to 8 cm across. It seems to require intervals of cool atmosphere to flower rather than a consistently uniform tropical heat.

Plate 18. *Dendrobium sanderae*
A native of the mountain regions of Luzon growing at an altitude of 1300 metres and more. There are two varieties, *D. sanderae* var. *major* with flowers 7 to 8 cm across and var. *parviflorum* with flowers only half this size. A smaller variety *surigaense* was discovered in 1951 collected from Surigao on the northern tip of Mindanao. All three varieties are available from Manila but presumably var. *surigaense* would need treating as a lowland plant.

Plate 19. *Dendrobium thyrsiflorum**
Another *Dendrobium* which should be in every collection. Easily grown and flowered in temperate regions with minor protection. It flowers prolifically in pendant racemes. It grows at 1500 metres in its natural habitat in Burma, India and Thailand.

Plate 20. A pot of *Dendrobium thyrsiflorum* in full flower.
Notice that the pot is not oversize which seems to be an important point in *Dendrobium* culture. The plant shown will remain in the pot shown for at least another season's growth.

Plate 21. *Dendrobium falcorostrum**
An Australian native plant which should be in every collection. It ranges from mid coast of eastern N.S.W. to south Queensland and will grow well out of doors in a Sydney climate. Flowering is from August to October. Like many Australian natives it looks well as a specimen plant and can be grown as shown in the Plate or in a shallow pot similar to that shown in **Plate 47**.

Plate 22. *Dendrobium linguiforme**
A very popular Australian native orchid widely distributed in N.S.W. and Queensland. This plant often grows on rocks in the Sydney area and I have seen it almost covering the sunny face

of a large rock. There is a tropical variety, var. *nugentii* which has larger leaves and other minor differences.

Plate 23. *Dendrobium tetragonum* var. *giganteum**
An Australian native from the tropics but one which seems to grow well at least as far south as Latitude 32°. It is rather pendulous in growth with slender stems which swell at their distal end and become four-sided.

Plate 24. *Dendrobium aemulum**
There are different forms of this Australian native orchid but the range is from southern N.S.W. to N. Queensland. Most forms are easy to grow outdoors in temperate climates but not an orchid for a pot as the root system needs to dry out thoroughly after watering.

Plate 25. *Oncidium flexuosum**
Tribe Cymbidieae, Sub-tribe Oncidiinae.
This plant from Brazil grows into quite large clumps outdoors in N.S.W. coastal climate. The photograph shows it in the author's garden fixed to a tree (*Leptospermum*). In this location it receives morning sun but is shaded from noon onwards.

Plate 26. A close-up of the flowers of the plant shown in **Plate 25**.
The young flower shoots seem to be a delicacy for possums so some wire protection may be needed when flower shoots appear.

Plate 27. *Ludisia discolor* var. *dawsoniana**
Tribe Erythrodeae, Sub-tribe Goodyerinae.
This has been included to show a typical 'Jewel' orchid grown mainly for its decorative leaves. This grows well in temperate climates if given the protection of a sun room or better. It has small white flowers and comes from Malaysia and Thailand. It is often known as *Haemaria* a name given to the genus in 1826 by Lindley. However, A. Richard named the genus in 1825 as *Ludisia* so this name must stand. There are several varieties with various leaf colours and veining.

Plate 28. Orchid Fruits
Those shown are from *Dendrobium speciosum*. Some capsules have split open to shed seed some of which has caught in the spider web.

Plate 29. *Phalaenopsis lueddemanniana*
Tribe Vandeae, Sub-tribe Sarcanthinae.
A popular species for those who have heated houses or live in the tropics. It is native to the Philippines and the one illustrated is a rather unusual yellow form.

Plate 30. A Phalaenopsis of unknown origin but popular with growers and in demand by florists.
The flowers shown are 12 cm across. Warm growing conditions are needed with a 17°C minimum.

Plate 31. *Phalaenopsis violacea*
This plant is native to Sumatra, Malaysia and Borneo. The plant shown is the Bornean variety, which has larger flowers than the others. A minimum temperature of 17°C is required with high humidity at all times.

Plate 32. *Phalaenopsis schilleriana*
This was previously written as *schillerana* but the 13th Botanical Congress decided that the spelling of epithets containing -er- should revert to -eriana. A very popular plant easy to obtain but needs 17°C. It comes from Luzon Island.

Plate 33. *Phalaenopsis stuartiana*
This flowers prolifically given warm winter conditions. From Mindanao Island in Philippines.

Plate 34. *Paphiopedilum parishii**
Sub-family Cypripedioideae
From Burma where it grows as an epiphyte unlike many others

of the genus which grow in leaf mould on the ground. Fairly easy to grow in temperate climates as its normal altitude is 1200 metres.

Plate 35. *Paphiopedilum argus**
A species from the Philippines growing at elevations up to 2300 metres. Easy to grow and easy to obtain. Never allow to dry out completely.

Plate 36. *Paphiopedilum callosum**
A species from Thailand and Cambodia found up to 1000 metres altitude. It is easy to grow and easy to obtain but may need some winter protection. Never allow to dry out completely. This grows quite well in a relative humidity of 70% or more.

Plate 37. *Paphiopedilum insigne**
The normal species with the dots and brown lip comes from Assam. The yellow plant is the same species but is variety *sanderae*. Both are easy to grow in temperate climates and no heating is needed. This is a green leaf type as distinct from the warmer growing tesselated leaf type.

Plate 38. *Renanthera monachica*
Tribe Vandeae, Sub-tribe Sarcanthinae.
A small growing *Renanthera*, quite rare in this genus of plants which tend to 'grow through the roof'. Flowers occur in October/November and are very long lasting. A species which needs warmth in winter but can grow in less light than its relatives which usually need direct intense sunlight. A native of the Philippines and was available in 1981 from a Townsville nursery.

Plate 39. *Rhynchostylis gigantea*
Tribe Vandeae, Sub-tribe Sarcanthinae.
A species ranging from Burma to Borneo and widely grown in Thailand. The flower colour is very variable from white with amethyst spots to the dark form shown here. Easy to grow in warm conditions and may currently be available from a Townsville orchid nursery.

Plate 40. *Trichoglottis philippinensis* var. *brachiata*
Tribe Vandeae, Sub-tribe Sarcanthinae.
A native of the Philippines often called the black orchid. There are several species in this genus all needing light and warmth.

Plate 41. *Vandanthe rothschildiana**
A hybrid between *Euanthe sanderiana* and *Vanda coerulea*. The latter, a cool growing orchid has passed this characteristic to the hybrid. This plant is sometimes called *Vanda rothschildiana*. It grows readily in a temperate climate without extra heat and should be in every collection.

Plate 42. *Vanda* Wongsi × *Ascocenda* Meda Arnold*
The purpose of this illustration is to show an intergeneric hybrid using small growing *Ascocentrum* parentage to reduce the size of a typical *Vanda*.

Plate 43. *Vanda tricolor* var. *suavis*
Tribe Vandeae, Sub-tribe Sarcanthinae
A noteable species from Java and Bali. Flowers August to November but requires high light and warmth.

Plate 44. *Vanda hindsii*
Widespread in New Guinea and extending into the Solomons. Quite rare in collections in Australia.

Plate 45. *Vanda stangeana*
A native from Assam growing at an altitude of 1500 metres. Rather rare and a collector's piece.

Plate 46. *Vanda* hybrids growing in a nursery in Bangkok. Some growers in Australia can grow individual plants of this quality but mostly the plants are not as good as those shown here. It needs constant high temperature, high humidity, high light and disease free conditions to obtain this result.

Plate 47. An orchid show in Sydney showing some Australian native plants grown as specimens in a shallow tray. This illustrates how many Australian native plants should be grown.

Plate 48. A corner of the author's glasshouse showing at the top left hand corner, plastic lining under the glass, a misting sprinkler just showing. The main purpose of the illustration is to show the long aerial roots (foreground and right hand side of picture) from plants hanging high up near the roof. Smaller plants are shown on wood and cork slabs suspended from vertical weldmesh. Space in a heated house, or any glasshouse is valuable and the goal is maximum space for plants and minimum space for humans.

9. PROPAGATION, SEXUAL & ASEXUAL

Definitions

Sexual propagation is the production of seeds by pollination of the stigma followed by fertilisation in the ovules of the ovary.

Self pollination occurs when the pollen of a flower is placed on to the stigma of the same flower or perhaps a flower of the same plant but is not extended further than this.

Cross pollination occurs when the pollen of one flower is placed on to the stigma of a flower in a different plant, albeit the same species or variety. If the process goes beyond this it is usually called hybridising, although the cross may not be fertile. However, the term is rather loosely used.

Asexual simply means not sexual and is, therefore, any form of producing progeny other than by seed. This includes division of the plant, the production of offsets (a side shoot usually from near the base of the parent plant), the production of aerial offsets (keiki, meaning a little one) along the upper parts of the stem.

Tissue propagation is also a form of asexual propagation as is protoplast culture when this latter method becomes a realistic proposition for orchids.

Sexual propagation

In nature, as explained in previous chapters and in Topic 3, the orchid needs to be supported by a fungus until it germinates and becomes established. Orchid seeds can still be sown on the top of existing pots of orchids where this fungus is likely to exist. Given favourable conditions the seed will germinate and grow. For many early hybridists this was the only method known for the germination and growth of seeds. Such haphazard methods would hardly be sufficient to meet present day demands of the commercial orchid industry. This largely owes its growth to Lewis Knudson, an American plant physiologist who in 1922 published a method for the asymbiotic germination of orchid seed. His method was to copy that of bacteriologists for the culture of bacteria. They provide a suitable source of carbon and nitrogen for the bacteria, place this into solution and add the necessary minerals such as magnesium, iron, etc. and add Agar to form the solution into a jelly, then bottle it, sterilise it and inoculate with bacteria. Usually the carbon source is a sugar and the nitrogen source either ammonium or nitrate.

Knudson used cane sugar as the carbon source as he considered the principal function of the fungus was to provide carbohydrate to the seed which does not contain any more food than a few oil droplets, so until germination takes place and photosynthesis commences the seed and embryonic plant needs outside support.

The Knudson C formula is given here purely to illustrate the type of mixture used to germinate orchid seed. It is not intended to be a reference for those people who wish to grow orchids from seed as far more specialised and comprehensive texts exist on this subject. (Refer Arditti J.A. (ed.) *Orchid Biology, reviews and perspectives,* Cornell University Press, 1977.)

Monobasic potassium phosphate	0.25 gram
Calcium nitrate	1.00 gram
Ammonium sulphate	0.50 gram
Magnesium sulphate	0.25 gram
Ferrous sulphate	0.025 gram
Manganese sulphate	0.0075 gram
Cane sugar	20.00 gram
Distilled water	1 litre
Agar	15 gram

This is a simple formula and today's orchid growers have added a wide range of substances to ensure better germination and growth. The growth medium is sterilised and placed in sterile flasks or bottles. If the orchid seed capsule has burst open the seed must also be sterilised and added in small quantities to each flask. If sterilisation has been effective the seeds will grow into plantlets; if not effective the crop will be spoiled by rapid fungal growth for fungi may also be cultured quite well in such a medium.

This method of propagation has made it possible for anyone and everyone to afford to buy small orchids and has given untold impetus to the industry.

It is not essential for every orchid enthusiast to be able to raise orchids from seeds. Some people do not desire to do so, others have neither the equipment nor the time. There are some very experienced growers who hand their seed over to other persons to sow into a flask on their behalf rather than go to the trouble of acquiring all the chemicals, apparatus and know-how to do the job themselves for just a few seed capsules per year and this approach really makes sense. Many commercial organisations will do the job for a modest cost, often on a no-result no-pay basis, or perhaps a small cover charge.

It is not intended in this chapter to list various seed raising media, although this makes for easy authorship, or to explain the process of seed raising. Although this is not very complex it needs to be explained in full to be worthwhile. Reference to the Australian Orchid Review for Australian readers will show that several organisations, which hopefully will call themselves 'Micropropagation Centres' rather than 'laboratories' will handle your seed. Other than this growers may purchase packets of ready made media for a few dollars, sufficient to make up one litre of media but one must be able to sterilise this and the containers for it. Some recent research in U.S.A. is being directed to including in the medium mixture, a substance which will inhibit fungal growth but not affect the germination of orchid seed. If this is successful and taken up by the media-providing industry, then it will simplify home growing of seed.

Before embarking on the project of growing orchids from seed or even of producing seed for someone else to grow, think carefully about it. Is the seed you have or anticipate, going to be worth growing on? If it is a hybrid seed you will indeed be lucky to get really worthwhile plants. Good hybrids are bred from carefully selected stock by persons who have had much training and experience in this field. Often this requires repeated cross-breeding and the weeding out of thousands of useless plants. Many growers just do not have the time, premises and equipment for this type of activity. Breeding new plants can be fun, if it is fun you want, but lots of labour goes with it, as plants take three years or more to show whether anything worthwhile has eventuated.

Many enthusiasts and commercial growers support the concept of conservation of plant species, both exotic and native. As a practical gesture they self-pollinate many species and grow and sell these seedlings rather than strip plants from the jungles and bush. Flasks of these may be purchased and contain between 6 and 30 plants each.

So instead of seed sowing techniques this section of this chapter will deal with pollination and fertilisation of the orchid flower as this activity is worth attempting just for experience and learning more about the anatomy of the plants. In Chapter 5 the anatomy of the plant was explained and illustrated so a brief re-look at the placement of the pollinia and stigmatic surface is in order. However, hours of studying paper work will not replace some practical experience with the flower. A toothpick is an excellent tool for pollination and a large magnifying glass, about ×3 or ×5 helps a lot unless your eyesight is keen.

Obtain an orchid flower, the larger the better for a start and set it in a secure and stable position, place a small white card under the column to catch falling pieces. Lift the anther cap with the point of the toothpick. This will show the pollinia inside and this will probably be in groups of 2, 4 or 8. The number of pollinia forms a very useful method of differentiating between genera, for example between Cattleya and Laelia and between Dendrobium and Eria, so the practice of lifting out and examining pollinia has some use other than pollinating flowers.

In some species any probing under the anther cap will result in the pollinia sticking to the toothpick by a sticky (viscid) disc attached to the pollinia stalks. In other species, e.g. Dendrobium, the pollinia are quite free and may tend to fall out and get lost easily. In this latter case, touching the tip of the toothpick on to the stigmatic surface which is sticky, and then on to the pollinia will help to secure them. Press the pollinia on to the stigmatic surface of the flower destined to become the female parent, where they will be covered with the sticky substance. The rest is up to the plant.

Fertilisation is not immediate, orchids are rather slow and it takes some time for the pollen tubes to grow down the column into the ovary, find the ovules and inject the gametes (sex cells) to fertilise the embryo. An orchid capsule may contain a million or more possible embryos and just how the pollen tubes and gametes find these and mate with them defies imagination. Not all seeds are fertile, usually those closer to the top of the ovary and the flower receive better attention from the pollen than those lower down.

The following list gives some idea of the time taken between pollination and fertilisation of some species.

Orchis (a geophyte)	2 weeks
Many geophytic orchids are very quick to fertilise	
Paphiopedilum insigne	14 weeks
Dendrobium species	10 to 14 weeks
Vanda sauvis	26 to 40 weeks
Cattleya species	6 weeks
Bulbophyllum species	8 weeks

However, the sepals and petals will wilt quickly or change colour and may be removed leaving only the flower stalk, topped by the ovary and column.

Storing pollen

For those who wish to cross hybridise it may be necessary to store the pollinia until the desired female parent flowers. Pollen may be stored and is usually viable for at least six months. It should be placed in a small sealed specimen bottle (3 cm × 0.7 cm). Dipping the sealing cap end of the specimen bottle in melted paraffin wax and letting solidify is a good method of sealing around the plastic cap. The specimen bottle(s) may then be placed in a larger jar, e.g. a jam jar, for storage and safety. No dehydrating agents, such as silica gel or calcium chloride, should be added as this causes the germination percentage to fall rapidly. Storage at about 7°C is advisable, particularly if the pollinia are to remain viable for 12 months. Storage temperatures of up to 20°C are satisfactory for most short term (6 months) storage but if facilities are available the bottom shelf of the domestic refrigerator seems a preferable storage place.

Obviously pollen should never be mixed with other pollen and only one set of pollinia should ever be placed on the one stigmatic surface. Always wait for the flower to mature before pollinating it, this is usually after it has been open for a few days.

Many epiphytes and geophytes will indulge in self-pollination so it may be necessary to remove the pollinia of these flowers as soon as it can be reached. However, this may cause immediate wilt and no further development of the flower, so some experimental work is needed.

The fruit

The time for the development of the orchid fruit which is a capsule (not a pod) varies with the genus. Some geophytes become ripe and burst open in a short period, others take 2 to 4 months and some, such as *Phalaenopsis* much longer.

At some stage in the development of the fruit, when the seed is still not ripe, the seed may be removed from the capsule (under sterile conditions) and sown in nutrient medium. This is 'green-seed-culture' and has two advantages in that the seed does not have to be subject to sterilisation which does nothing to improve its viability, and the grower does not have to wait so long for the capsule to ripen. As a rough guide the capsule is ready for culture in about half the time taken to fully ripen. There are also two disadvantages; all the seeds must be used at the one sowing so distribution is limited and the risk of failure is high should the capsule be harvested before fertilisation of the ovules occurs.

If allowed to remain on the plant the capsule will eventually open up and disperse the seed (**Plate 28**).

A plant which is required to nurse fruits to maturity puts a lot of effort into this task to the detriment of new growth of the plant; therefore, unless you require the seeds it is better to cut the old flower stem and fruits off the plant so that it can break into new growth.

Asexual propagation

Competency in this is essential for all orchid growers to control that *Cattleya* or *Coelogyne* or whatever which is climbing out of its pot and becoming too difficult to handle.

Before recommending that large plants be broken up the other point of view should be mentioned. Many plants, particularly Australian native plants, such as *Dendrobium kingianum*, *Dendrobium gacilicaule*, *Sarcochilus hartmannii* and others make splendid specimen plants when grown in large saucer type pots. Each year the plant expands in size and such a specimen is indeed a great sight when in flower. Other plants, e.g. *Rhynchostylis*, can grow into specimens and produce a large number of racemes. The plant is not always tidy and vegetatively it may dismay a gardener but the yearly flowering is worth it. So do not be in too much of a hurry to divide up plants.

However, we are speaking of propagation which implies multiplication of the plant. If the plant has been given a cultivar name, perhaps as a result of an award, this name should be attached to all of the pieces detached and grown on (refer to Chapter 7).

Sympodial growth

In this type of growth pseudobulbs arise in succession from a rhizome and in many cases three or four pseudobulbs may overhang the pot and these may be conveniently cut off and used as one division. Never try to propagate from less than 3 pseudobulbs (four are preferred). A lesser number may be used but the plant takes years to develop if it ever does. The time to take the 'cutting' is when a new growth is evident, about 2 cm long, but new roots have not grown. If this is an epiphyte and is destined to grow in a pot place it on *top of the pot* with the new growth to the centre and the cut edge against the pot rim. Do not bury the rhizome or pseudobulbs, most of the old roots may be cut off, leave just a few to assist anchorage in the pot. New roots will grow but any shifting of the plant in relation to the potting mixture will easily damage these; hence firm staking is necessary.

Keep the potting mixture slightly damp which will ultimately encourage root growth to enter the mix.

To protect the plants from excess water loss keep in a cool shady place and mist spray the leaves and pseudobulbs twice on sunny days. When potting epiphytic plants into a medium or large size pot it is a saving in the substrate if an unbroken clay pot is placed in the bottom of the new pot in an inverted position. Clay pots of 7.5 cm and 10 cm are most useful and the hole in the base of the pot may be used to hold a stake in position to give some rigidity.

If an entire orchid plant is to be subdivided it is useful to cut through the rhizome in several places to give 3- or 4-pseudobulb divisions, and leave it in the pot undisturbed until new shoots appear. The several plants may then be removed and potted as described. This procedure can only be done with those plants having a sufficiently long interval between pseudobulbs.

Years ago, before tissue culture, growers were forced to obtain as many plants as possible from a single pseudobulb, e.g. *Cymbidium*, but this technique of 'back-bulb' reproduction has largely been superseded by tissue culture and even expensive plants can be divided as above.

Monopodial growth

New plants may arise from offshoots coming from near the base of the plant. If it is desired to propagate these do not attempt to do so before the new growth has sent out one root, preferably two roots or more. A sharp knife will separate the young plant from its parent.

Phalaenopsis at times produce young plants from the flower stems instead of flowers. Do not separate these from the plants too early. Young orchid plants are not easy to raise so the more robust they are when forced into an independent existence, the better.

Most monopodials can be cultivated on cork slabs which ensures that the roots are well drained. If pot culture is necessary the root tips are very delicate and should not be forced into pots or allowed to rub against charcoal or bark. Firm staking is essential, with misting and shading until the roots have decided where they will go and what they will adhere to. It is very easy to lose a young plant if this point is not watched carefully.

While monopodials can be grown into specimen plants some offshoots will fairly rapidly produce another offshoot and then refuse to go any further, neither growing nor flowering. If this condition persists for a year, separate the two growths if both have roots and at least one should then show progressive growth, the original offshoot may not grow and can be discarded.

Paphiopedilum

These multiply by sending out new growth from the base. It is very inadvisable to remove these at any stage. Apart from this a full pot of *Paphiopedilum* in flower is gratifying to everyone. After many years the plant may grow too large in which case it can usually be split into just two or three good size divisions, repotted and grown on.

Aerial Offsets (Keikis)

These are very prevalent on *Dendrobium* and may be allowed to remain on the stems and grow. They will eventually flower just as well as the main stem flowers. If it is desired to remove these to grow on, this should not be done until the keiki is about 15 cm long. The roots tend to cling to the main stem so may be damaged on removal. If the young plant is to be grown on a cork slab remove the keiki and part of the old stem to which the roots are clinging and secure the lot on to a slab.

Fertiliser

New roots are very easily damaged by fertiliser, particularly solid particles of it. To assist in keeping a young subdivision alive and well, foliar fertilising is recommended using a soluble fertiliser at about 1/4 normal strength sprayed weekly on leaves and pseudobulbs and roots if existing.

Tissue Propagation

Propagation by this method is a specialist task, even more so than growing from seed. Any grower who wishes to carry out this work should consult those publications describing methods and culture media. The normal orchid enthusiast is not usually anxious to obtain large quantities of any one plant, quantities for which he must find room and pots to grow on for years. This type of work is better left to those commercial organisations having the space, labour and sales for these plants. These are sold as mericlones, in flasks or as plants a year or two out of the flask. Recently many mericlone plants have reached maturity and have been found to be anything but true copies of their parents. It was once thought that a mericloned plant, being vegetatively produced must end up as a true copy of the parent plant. Some of the plants flower poorly or not at all, others have distorted flowers with twisted parts or even more parts than the flower should have.

Nevertheless, the purchase of mericloned plants can give you some good stock but proceed carefully, buy one or two at a time and see if these turn out well enough to extend your range.

10. DEFLASKING & COMMUNITY POTS

Young orchid plants pass through three stages in their life before becoming adult flowering plants. These are:
1. The flask stage from seeds.
2. The community pot stage from the flask.
3. The 5 cm pot stage from the community pot.

Plants may be purchased at any of these stages and the purpose of this chapter is to cover the removal from the flask or bottle, i.e. deflasking and the planting into community pots and their care.

Flasked plants come in two types:
1. Those in which the seed was sown.
2. Those in which the plants have been transplanted from the seedling flask.

For the home orchid enthusiast the second type is preferred. The number of plants in a transplanted flask is less than the original seedling flask but quite sufficient to satisfy the needs of the home grower. Also the plants are more uniform after transplanting and the discards will be fewer.

Before plants are removed from the flask prepare the community pots. These can be ordinary 12 to 15 cm pots, squat type preferred, or seed flats used by commercial growers for garden seedlings. The orchid roots are going to cling to the material used in the pots and may be broken on removal if the material is too large and heavy. Very 'fine', i.e. small pieces, bark with pieces no larger than 0.5 cm and some finely chopped up sphagnum moss may be used as a substrate. Some small pieces of charcoal can also be advantageously mixed in with the bark. The charcoal holds moisture in its crevices and ensures some humidity around the roots even when the bark dries out.

This substrate should be pasteurised a few days before use. This can be done by steaming of a small amount in a pressure cooker or steamer by placing the substrate in a shallow container. Usually steaming at 100°C for 20 minutes is sufficient it being unnecessary to pasteurise under pressure. Another method is to wet the substrate thoroughly and place it on a flat tray in an oven set to 110°C (230°F) for 20 to 30 minutes. Some people are satisfied to drench the substrate thoroughly with a fungicidal solution using Benlate, Captan or Copper Oxychloride and allowing this to drain and dry out. With either of the two methods using heat the substrate material should be ventilated in a room for several hours stirring with a clean fork. At other times keep it covered to minimise re-infection.

If the flasks have arrived in good condition there is no need for immediate deflasking. The flasks may be placed in a cool shady spot. Although some light is required too much may burn up the seedlings. If the contents of the flask looks a mess, due to rough transport, deflasking should be done at once.

Some bottles and flasks have a wide mouth allowing a knife blade to be slipped into the flask and the seedlings lifted out. For narrow necked bottles one needs a piece of stiff wire with the end bent into a U to hook out the seedlings. They are fairly tough despite their delicate appearance.

The seedlings should be scooped, hooked or otherwise removed from the flask directly into a basin of water, not too cold, about 22 to 25°C does nicely. Here they are washed to remove all of the agar gel. Leaving this on the roots will only promote fungal growth. Several changes of water may be needed to ensure clean plants.

If the seedlings are from a non-transplanted flask they will be very variable in size and need to be sorted into large, medium and small sizes in three bowls of water. Never let seedlings dry out. Sorting is preferred at this stage rather than later on in the community pots, where it is desirable for all seedlings in a pot to progress uniformly.

Before planting, the seedlings are immersed in a fungicide solution of your choice and then planted immediately into the community pots. This is a tiring task so you may decide to use only the large plants or large and medium, discarding the small sizes.

The pots should be filled to 1/3 of their depth with drainage material, such as clay crocks, and the seedling substrate added and the whole lot wet and allowed to drain.

Commence sowing near the rim of the pot or back edge of a flat using a pencil or similar device to make a hole in the substrate. Insert the seedling without breaking the roots and cover with the substrate. Keep the junction of the root and stem just above substrate level. Some roots will fit into the hole easily, others will want to go anywhere but the desired place. Let them do so even if they are on top of the substrate. Place seedlings 2 or 3 cm apart, depending on size and work around the pot edge gradually progressing towards the centre.

After sowing, spray with a very dilute water soluble fertiliser using enough to cover a 2 cent piece to four litres of water. Make out a label and insert into the pot.

Community pots or flats must be kept in a warm, damp atmosphere and are best placed in a plant humicrib made from a suitable box with a glass or clear polythene cover on top. Ideally the minimum night temperature of 16°C is needed for good growth so an electric blanket or other heater should be arranged to maintain this temperature.

At first the seedlings need low light intensity, similar to a living room. Strong light will be detrimental at this stage so use a shade cloth over the box if necessary. After a few months, depending on the growing season, increase the light intensity twofold. The cover on the box should be lifted during part of the day to ensure air change. The seedlings must be made to grow. If they remain static they are likely to reverse growth and die off. The raising of young orchid seedlings is not always easy. To promote growth mist spray every day to wet the plants and the container, to maintain humidity, perhaps twice on a hot dry day when the lid is open. Fertilise as above once a week and as the plants grow increase the fertiliser concentration by 2.

Fungal attacks can still occur and if the young plants are seen to keel over at soil level or look brown, remove the pot, pull out the dead or sickly plants and douse the pot with a fungicide solution. The use of several pots instead of a single seed tray has the advantage of confining any fungal attack to a few plants rather than let it rampage through the lot.

Snails and slugs are a real pest but if the pots and flats are properly boxed up with a good fitting cover these are not a serious problem. However, some Baysol around the seedling box is a worthwhile precaution.

After spending a year in a community pot the small plants are ready to be individually potted into 5 cm pots. However, this should not be done until early spring or summer as it is unwise to disturb the plants when growth is minimal.

The plants are still young, only two to three years of age so require some coddling, particularly at first. Treat them in just the same way as they were treated in the community pots. A somewhat coarser substrate may be used, larger pieces of bark or charcoal for epiphytes, for others use a substrate as set down in Chapter 6. Depending on the time of the year when transplanting was done, these young plants will take six to twelve months to establish. After this period and with new growth commencing they may be treated a little less carefully.

After all this many people may prefer to buy their plants already established in 5 cm pots at about $2.50 each. This saves one to two years of delicate growing time. One does not get as many plants but perhaps one or two of each will meet your needs.

Additional notes of interest

It has been reported that seedling growth is much accelerated by watering the seedlings with one millilitre of 'Formula 20' placed in one litre of water to which is added seven grams of sugar. This is applied every two weeks to seedlings which have been established in community pots for a month. Growers may care to try out this procedure on a few plants to test its efficacy. The sugar will most certainly act as a carbon source for fungal growth but whether you have good or bad fungi present is open to chance.

Some 20 years ago a report came from Indonesia that beer, fed to seedlings once per week for six weeks at the rate of 5 ml per pot greatly encouraged growth. As an alternative spray the seedlings twice per week with a mixture of beer and water at a 1:1 ratio for a period of six weeks. The significance of the six week limit is not understood.

Further experiments made in Malaysia using diluted beer as a foliar spray appeared to be very effective and many local party goers may like to use the left overs to advance our knowledge of fertilising adult orchid plants.

11. PESTS & DISEASES

In any monoculture crop, that is where the same type of plant is grown in a confined area, there is always the possibility that any disease present will spread rapidly and the insect population will multiply readily. In nature, plants of the same type are more widely distributed which, along with natural predators, keeps the spread of the pests and diseases under reasonable control. However, one only has to walk through our own bush to see that many trees and shrubs are partly given over to the support of insect colonies. This is nature's way; all must live but the orchid grower does not take too kindly to this concept. Control is exercised by housing the plants in some protective covering and spraying. Few natural predators are possible but one could suggest the odd insect-eating spider and a few lizards could well be on the glasshouse staff to keep watch on this aspect.

The approach to pest and disease control has been to spray with a toxic or inhibiting chemical and a vast amount of money has been spent on this lucrative market on the basis that we have to feed our growing human population by preventing excessive crop losses.

Many articles have been written on chemical control of orchid problems and no doubt the advice is good. However, many chemicals for pest and disease control are not available at your local garden store and if you do find them, they are often in lots of 5 litres or more or in large packs, both expensive and long lasting. Of course, many large orchid collections warrant being treated as a small commercial nursery but the object of this chapter is to advise growers with less than 1000 plants of various genera.

With the advent of the Pesticides Act and the registration of various garden chemicals for specific purposes it is unwise for any garden writer to recommend any particular chemical for any purpose not specified on the label. Additionally the requirements and registration is a State matter so what is permissible in one State is not in another. So if you are looking for something to solve your pest and disease problems—read the label. You are also required to do this for your own protection.

Personal protection is something which cannot be treated too lightly. One product noted recently was marked as 'Anti choline esterase' which is fine if the purchaser has any idea what 'choline esterase' is or does. So how to interpret this? The nerve pulse travels down a nerve fibre or axon and at the end of this a chemical called acetyl choline is released to pass on the nerve impulse to the adjacent nerve cell across the synaptic cleft between the axon and the cell. The acetyl choline having done its job is broken down by choline esterase and until this is done no further impulses can cross the synaptic cleft. So anything which is anti-choline-esterase can have a serious effect on the correct functioning of the nervous system. This can affect the proper functioning of muscles, very serious if these are concerned with lung action. The substance functions by affecting the muscles of the insect; uncontrolled muscles cause convulsions even to the squeezing of organs out of the insect's body.

Perhaps the use of this type of term could eventually have more impact on the user than just stating that the spray was an organo-phosphorus compound, which is also fairly meaningless. While on the subject of protection the most vulnerable parts of the body are where the skin is thinnest. These are the conjunctiva or skin of the eye and the lung tissue. So goggles and face mask, as used by many nurseries, are necessary equipment if you propose to do much spraying around of chemicals. Absorption also occurs through the body skin so rubber gloves are a 'must' and tropical dress is out; no shorts or thongs and wear a long sleeve shirt.

The Pests

Slugs and snails could well head the list but these are a problem for every gardener. Possums could also be added as the flower buds of orchids growing on trees in the garden, appear to be delicious.

Other than these there appear to be four principal pests but these may vary from district to district: 1. mealy bug 2. two spotted mite 3. scale insects 4. the orchid (*Dendrobium*) beetle (see **Plate 10**).

1. **Mealy bug** is rather a pest in glasshouses where they inhabit the junction of leaf and stem where it is difficult for a water spray to penetrate. If only a few plants are infested a simple remedy is a bottle of methylated spirit and a pipette dropper. The methylated spirit when dropped on to the insect strips off its protective coating and hopefully dehydrates it. By inspecting plants regularly this pest can usually be kept in check. If a spray is needed

'Lebaycid' has been found satisfactory but no doubt there are others.

2. **The two-spotted mite** (often called redspider) thrives in hot, dry no-wind conditions which hardly seems to describe a good orchid environment. The mites usually appear in September/October and multiply at a great rate if unchecked. In the author's glasshouse the humidity does not fall below 70% and there is air movement at most times. If the temperature rises so does the humidity (it is arranged that way) and two-spotted mites have never been seen, so in this type of culture the conditions prevent infestation.

For a spray, if needed use Kelthane® or any other miticide from your garden store. If these mites are a real problem biological control is a possibility. Biocontrol, of Warwick in Queensland 4370, can supply a domestic pack of a Predatory Mite which feeds exclusively on the two-spotted mite. However, it is useless introducing these unless you have a good population of two-spotted mite for the predators to feed upon.

3. **Scale insects.** These can be a problem on all types of orchids where they feed under the leaves. A scale called Boisduval scale is also a pest if allowed to multiply. The males are white, elongate with three ridges down the back. The females are disc shaped, flat and light brownish.

If the plants are inspected regularly the simplest method of eradication is to wipe off the scale with a rag soaked in methylated spirit or even use your finger nail to remove the scale. In a bad infestation use Rogor with white oil added and be sure to spray well under the leaves.

4. **The orchid beetle.** This beetle, about one cm long, believes in using gravity to assist his escape route. He will invariably fall downwards if capture appears imminent, so place one hand underneath his perch and attempt capture with the other. As the beetle falls into the strategically placed hand it can be captured and disposed of. A general purpose insecticide can be used if necessary. The larval stage, a grub, eats out the interior of *Dendrobium* stems, so if an infested stem is detected it should be removed and destroyed immediately.

Before leaving the subject of pests just a word on the development of resistance to sprays. It is frequently stated or implied that the continued use of a chemical for a long time causes individual insects to build up a resistance to it and pass this on to their progeny. This is not so. There is only one direction of inheritance and that is from DNA and the base sequence in the chromosomes, outwards. There is no mechanism for the environment to modify the genetic make up of an organism; that is, there is no inward path to modify the base sequence in the chromosome and so alter the inherited properties.

Insects, as individuals, do not develop resistance to chemical spray. There may be just a few individuals in a population which are *genetically different* in one respect from the others. Perhaps they are able to survive the muscular contractions brought about by organo-phosphorus compounds. When most of the population are killed off these few survive and produce a population now resistant to compounds of this type. That is, the new population has acquired a resistance by being bred from parents originally possessing this characteristic, and who survived the onslaught.

To overcome this there is not much point in trying to gain control once more by the use of an organo-phosphorus compound related to the one used previously. One must change to another type such as the chlorinated hydrocarbons (e.g. DDT) or the carbamates.

Fungal Diseases (including bacterial)

Fungal diseases are probably more cause for concern in orchid culture than the pests. If left without control the disease may readily spread throughout the house. The diagnosis of the actual fungus is rarely necessary except that some fungicides are rather specific for certain organisms.

Perhaps the most serious problem encountered is from two fungi, both water moulds, called *Pythium* and *Phytophthera*, so similar that the recognition of these as separate genera is due only to precedent. In fact modern taxonomy tends to classify these two genera as heterotrophic protista, rather than fungi, grouping them as water moulds and slime moulds, the latter being terrestrial in habit.

The term water mould gives some clue to the way these organisms spread. Damp ground and damp pot substrate causes the organisms to multiply rapidly. *Pythium* is the greatest enemy of seedlings in community pots (see Chapter 10). It is also injurious to roots, stems and leaves of many orchids including *Cymbidium*, *Cattleya* and *Paphiopedilum*. Its companion water mould, *Phytophthera* is similarly devastating and both may be treated without differentiation by a fungicide Fongarid®. This is systemic in action and is watered into the soil. Directions given by the manufacturer should be followed.

Leaf spots are perhaps easier to control than stem

and root rots as the latter sometimes gain a hold before they or their effects are seen. A variety of fungi cause leaf spots and are best treated with a suitable fungicide for ornamentals. The author has used Benlate, Copper oxychloride and Captan on orchids without any phytotoxic effect. This latter point is most important. When trying a new fungicide or insecticide, spray a few orchids only, during the hot part of the day and check the plants in 3 to 5 days time for possible damage. Do not try for a fast job by mixing a lot of chemicals together as one may reduce the effect of the others. Spray one at a time for a specific problem notwithstanding the Compatibility Charts.

One can always adopt the surgeon's solution. If it is diseased cut it out! Such action usually helps to control the spread of the disease but the cut surface remaining on the plant should be flooded with methylated spirit to kill the surface cells and prevent infection from another source. However, before cutting or disturbing a diseased leaf or stem place as much of it as possible into a bag, then cut it and destroy the lot. Fungal diseases are spread by spores, which are sitting on the leaf surface waiting for some activity to disperse them. If these shake off and fall on another plant where there is a little moisture, the disease spreads.

Bacterial diseases causing leaf spots cannot be controlled by fungicides and surgery is the solution. Some mercurial compounds have been used with success but this should only be done by those used to handling toxic chemicals with a full knowledge of their composition.

The bacterium *Pseudomonas aeruginosa* is a common pathogen found in soil and sewage and while not exactly aggressive, it is responsible for several plant diseases including leaf spot on orchids, in particular *Phalaenopsis*, *Cattleya* and *Vanda*. The symptoms of bacterial leaf infection are varied, perhaps a brown watery area with an irregular yellow boundary and with brown droplets oozing out, or can be squeezed out, of the leaf. At other times the leaf tip has alternate dark and light bands across it, looks watery except where complete necrosis has set in at the top; here it is brittle and dry.

Flower spotting occurs under conditions of high humidity, with poor air circulation, particularly on *Phalaenopsis*, *Cattleya* and *Cymbidium*, different species and hybrids displaying varying susceptibility. Two fungi are usually responsible, *Botrytis cinerea* and *Sclerotina fuckeliana*. Attack most frequently occurs on flowers past their prime so to prevent spread of the disease, remove these from the plant, increase ventilation and raise the temperature to reduce relative humidity. Spray control is difficult without damaging the good flowers but try Dacomil 2787® repeating in seven days time.

Virus

Perhaps one of the most discussed disease problems of orchids is viral infection. There is no cure and infected plants should be burnt. However, against this drastic action there is always the question—is it a virus or isn't it? *Cymbidium* cultivars have received most attention in this country because of the need for virus free flowers for the export market. It is difficult to be certain unless flowers have severe colour breaks when one can be reasonably sure and destroy the plant. Another symptom is irregular yellow areas along the leaves which may later turn black. However, other factors can cause this; hence the question. If very young leaves have this irregular yellow mosaic then one can reasonably suspect that virus is present. Plants can be purchased from recognised orchid nurseries with assurance that they are virus free, however, beware of making purchases from unknown private growers who may unwittingly off-load infected plants. This can occur when the collection of a deceased person is sold off. Fortunately the close watch kept on this disease has reduced its incidence but it could get out of hand rapidly if infected plants are allowed to circulate.

The virus is present in the plant sap so cutting instruments should be dipped in methylated spirit and flamed before proceeding to cut another plant. Sap on the fingers may also result in virus transfer.

The only really conclusive test of virus presence is to innoculate orchid plant sap into known indicator plants, or conduct serological tests or make an electron microscope examination. All of these are beyond the scope of this book.

Culture

Improper methods of culture can also produce disease conditions of the plant. Cultural practices are discussed in Chapter 6 but a brief review of ailments not caused by organisms is appropriate to this chapter. Overwatering in pots tends to exclude the air and keep the roots in a sodden condition. It is really a disease of pot culture and does not occur when epiphytes are grown on wooden or bark slabs. Poor air movement also inhibits drying out of roots and substrates and is a common feature of poorly vented glasshouses (see Topic 1). Under-watering can also be a problem as it can be difficult to wet slabs, or the water just runs around the bark in pots without wetting it. This can be remedied by two or three light waterings spaced about half hour apart. The author uses a misting system to water, the amount of wetness being measured electronically and if the first watering is insufficient a further two repeat waterings are allowable, spaced 30 minutes apart and given automatically as dictated by the water sensor. This system seems to be more effective than just one watering for a longer period.

Excess light means excess heat developed in the leaves and some orchids, especially *Cattleya* are prone to leaf burn when subject to excess light perpendicular to the leaf surface. A cool breeze may offset this excessive light rather than using shading.

Nutrient deficiency

Orchids are slow growing plants and have a minimum need for nutrients but this does not mean starvation. If anything, growers may tend to overfeed, particularly if used to the culture of other garden plants, so deficiency problems seldom arise. A bark substrate requires frequent applications of a nitrogenous fertiliser, not so much to feed the orchid but to feed the fungi decomposing the bark, otherwise the plant itself is starved of nitrogen. Nitrogen is a mobile element in the plant so it is transferred readily from old growth to new growth when there is not enough for all. The old growth changes from green to yellow and this progresses upwards or towards the new growth. The leaves fall off prematurely.

Other deficiency symptoms may occur if the grower is suddenly aware of a nitrogen deficiency and heaps in nitrogen and nothing else. When correcting a deficiency use a fertiliser containing all nutrients required; even molybdenum may be necessary if the fertiliser is high in nitrates which require molybdenum for processing into a useable form within the plant.

Salting up

This is often the result of over enthusiastic fertilising without cleaning out the substrate with water between fertiliser applications. The roots will stop growing, often developing a black tip. Although the fertiliser regime is sometimes quoted as being 'very little and often' the failure to wash out the substrate adequately, be it a pot or a slab, results in the accumulation of fertiliser salts. This concentration causes ex-osmosis (reverse water flow) at the root tip and sometimes its plasmolysis (see **Fig. 5-1**). Some growers alternate fertilisers of inorganic salts and organic material (e.g. Fish emulsion) to minimise salt build-up.

A complete treatise on orchid plant protection and pathology can hardly be covered in a short chapter. Various agricultural chemical manufacturers and the Department of Agriculture provide excellent pamphlets on plant protection, usually gratis, and although essentially for gardeners, orchid growers can obtain a lot of useful information from these.

TOPIC 1.   THE GLASSHOUSE

The two chapters on 'Housing the Plants' and 'Substrates and Culture' contain information which is introductory to this subject and should be studied in conjunction with this Topic.

In order to grow a wider range of plants in either warm temperate or cool temperate climates a glasshouse can become a necessity depending both on your winter climate and the species in which you are interested. In recent time there has been a shift away from some of the species which mandatorily require a lot of warmth in favour of the cooler growing types. This move has been prompted largely by the rising cost of fuel for established houses.

This Topic will, among other quantitative data, introduce the reader to the Solar Glasshouse particularly for those able to construct a new glasshouse. A Solar Glasshouse is not the same sort of thing as placing a solar hot water service near the house and using this to heat water and circulate this through the house. Many investigators, particularly in the U.S.A. have tried this system mainly because the bits and pieces were readily available for immediate research. While the system works satisfactorily the capital outlay was excessive in respect of large commercial glasshouses hence not recommended. There appears to have been very little done on the costing basis for the small amateur glasshouse and anyone with a spare solar hot water service lying around may like to do this work.

As one team of researchers stated 'Solar energy is not free. Since the initial cost is large compared to the operating cost, it is important to estimate the life of the system and the value of fuel saved over the period. In determining the fuel saved, do not assume that a given system will supply all or a major portion of your heating requirements'. (Baird and Waters, 'Hortscience' Vol 14 (2).)

Whether you intend to buy a glasshouse or build your own the floor will still be your responsibility and is a suitable subject to commence discussion. A layer of sand as the base topped with a layer of 'road base' makes an excellent floor and has the added merit of being cheap. The layers should be a minimum of 5 cm and preferably thicker up to say 15 cm. This type of floor allows the water to permeate through without leaving puddles and it also retains enough water to provide some humidity in the glasshouse. The black road-base material also absorbs heat from the sunlight falling on it during winter months and releases this heat into the air at night. Avoid a concrete floor for the same reasons as given in 'Housing the Plants'.

If you live in a frost prone area it will help to conserve heat loss through the floor if 30 cm wide × 5 cm thick polyurethane 'planks' or batts are buried edge on around the periphery of the floor. This minimises heat loss from the warm floor to the cold frosty ground outside. Too much emphasis cannot be laid on the conservation of heat in the design and construction of a new glasshouse for modifications are difficult after the house is up and functioning.

If the 'half wall' type of house is used (and this is highly recommended for orchid culture) it will also store heat and release this to both the inside and outside. Such a wall requires a concrete foundation of sorts which minimises heat escape from the floor to the external soil but it is still useful to place polyurethane 'planks' around the foundation.

Selection of a Glasshouse

Most of the commercially available glasshouses for home use in this country are built on the English or north European lines. The glass-to-floor type of house with its gabled roof at about 35° seems to have been designed to gain most of its light from radiant energy reflected from an overcast sky-dome rather than by direct radiation from the sun.

Consider the sky-dome as a hemisphere resting on the flat earth. On a heavily overcast day there will be no direct radiation from the sun; all light will be scattered, so entry into the glasshouse will be from all directions of the azimuth and zenith. The light intensity will probably be no greater than 1/10th of full sunlight. A bright overcast day gives some direct radiation, say up to 25% with 75% scattered radiation with some 1/2 to full sunlight intensity again requiring the glasshouse to have an 'all-round' looking aspect.

When the day is partly cloudy we receive some direct sunlight with some scattered light, say 30 to 40% from the clouds depending on their coverage of the dome. The light intensity through an 'all-round' house can be quite high. On a clear bright day such as we have in Australia during winter, the direct radiation is 90% with little scattered radiation, so the 'all-round' looking house is not needed and in fact can contribute to unwanted heat-loss.

A great disadvantage of the European style glass-to-floor, gabled roof style is its high inside temperature in Australian summers and considerable cooling is needed for optimum plant growth. Apart from these considerations the house is not high enough for orchid culture. It is usually limited to 2.1 metres at the top of the gable whereas a minimum height of 3 metres is needed if a large range of plants is to be grown. This height allows for a 'hang bar' close to the roof so that large, light loving, epiphytic orchids can be hung on this and their root systems allowed to trail down to floor or bench level (see **Plate 48**).

The half-wall type of house is a better buy as this can usually be supported on a wall height of your own choosing. It may be necessary to rehang the door, or even replace it, if it is made of metal (heat loss) but this is not too difficult. Those firms selling glasshouses seem reluctant to tell their prospective amateur purchasers about their larger houses so it may be necessary to badger the sales organisation to obtain data on their better types of glasshouses.

The other alternative, and a very much better one is to design and build your own house. The building part need not be done yourself, although there is a lot of fun and interest in so doing, but the building being done to your requirements is the important point.

This Topic will deal with many of the factors pertinent to glasshouse management such as temperature, cooling, humidity and so on but firstly the concept of a Solar Glasshouse will be explored and the prospective designer of a new glasshouse may like to consider the possibilities of this.

The principles of the Solar House are very simple; absorb as much heat as possible during a sunny winter's day, store this and release it at night, have high insulation against heat loss and absorb as little heat as possible during the warmer months. The prime consideration to accomplish this is the angle of the sun's rays in winter and summer. Refer to Appendix 1 for sun angle data. Consider a location at latitude 35°S, the vertical angle of the sun from 8 am to 4 pm will vary from 10° to 34° and back to 10° during the winter months. The design of the house should, therefore, allow maximum penetration of the sun's rays at these vertical angles. At this same latitude during mid-summer the vertical sun angles will be from 60° to 76° and back to 60° during the hottest part of the day. So by adopting a configuration shown in **Fig. T1-1** the glass allows maximum penetration of light in winter while keeping out the high intensity rays of summer.

Fig. T1-1 is a theoretical diagram only, showing the light and shade in a saw-toothed roof house. It is not a construction diagram. One may visualise this as a sectional side elevation of a glasshouse, oriented north and south, with the eastern wall removed and viewed from ground level looking inside the house from the eastern side. One can see all the bands of light and shade, the latter being shown cross hatched.

The only glass panels in the roof are vertical, the remainder of the roof is made of opaque material, such as timber, fibro sheet or whatever and preferably well insulated to avoid excess heat loss. Double glazing is desirable and does not present a difficult fitting problem.

These vertical panels admit only narrow shifting beams of light in summer but as the saw tooth angle is 27° (approximately) the entry of winter sunlight is maximised and floods the interior. If this theory is to be applied to latitudes other than 35° then the saw tooth angle must be adjusted to a suitable value. Refer to Appendix 1 for vertical sun angles in winter at various latitudes. Latitude changes will affect the pitch angle of the saw tooth hence the height of the glass panels, so the applied theory will result in slightly different constructional configuration.

The northern wall is mostly all glass (some vertical support pillars are necessary, the number depending on the width and material used). The high angle of incidence (68°) in summer en-

sures that most radiation is reflected away, only a small amount enters the house. However, the low angle winter radiation effectively passes through the glass. If necessary a shade cloth blind may be used over this glass wall in summer.

Any additional heat storage such as rocks, water tanks or jars or pipes containing circulating water are not shown in the diagram being left to the ingenuity and needs of the builder.

Although the diagram has been scaled at 1 cm = 30 cm this is for proportional and angular considerations only and small variations will be needed for different angles of sunlight.

The roof and southern wall may be made of any solid substances such as fibro sheet spaced by 75 mm using 75 mm × 50 mm timber, the spaces between timbers being filled with fibreglass batts.

The light entering the house must be stored and this can be done in water or in rocks. In some experimental houses 500 × one gallon black plastic (square) containers have been stored against the insulated rear wall of the house. These absorb heat during the day and radiate it at night. Heat transfers from a hot body to a colder body or area, at a rate determined by the difference in temperatures between these until finally both bodies or volumes of air or whatever, are at the same temperature. As the two temperatures approach each other there is very little quantity of heat transferred, so practically the hot source needs to be some 6 or 7°C higher than the volume being heated. Generally, rather than rely on diffusion of the heat, it is preferable to use a slow fan to ensure an air flow over the heat source.

In another experimental glasshouse a 500 gallon water tank was installed under the benches, the sides of the tank were ribbed or corrugated and the whole placed into an insulating jacket. A fan secured to this jacket sucked air in from the hot house passing this air through a large diameter polythene tube stretched out over the water in the tank. The water absorbed the heat via its metal tank as long as the incoming air was at a higher temperature than the water. As the glasshouse air became colder than the water, heat was given up by the latter to re-heat

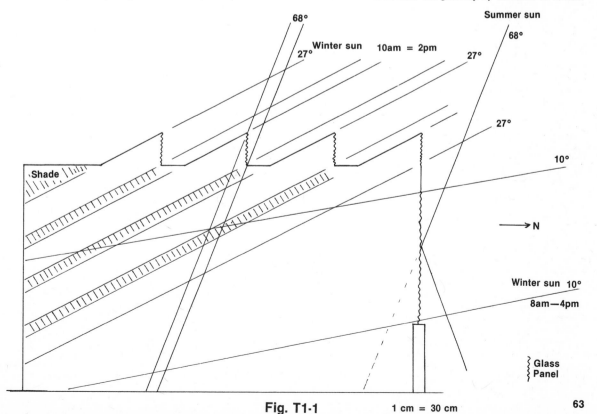

Fig. T1-1 1 cm = 30 cm

the glasshouse air. The insulating jacket was made from 19 mm styrofoam. Even though some leakage may have occurred from the tank this was not lost, as it would have been if the tank had been located externally.

The use of a rock-pile to store heat is worthy of consideration, especially for glasshouses yet to be built. This can be done by building an annexe on to the already well insulated southern wall of the glasshouse, this annexe to have a volume equal to 15% of the glasshouse. The actual rock-pile needs to have a volume equal to 8% of the glasshouse volume but a space is needed both above and below the pile for air movement. A slot is placed in the rear wall of the house parallel to the roof and close to the top of a container.

A similar slot and parallel to the top one is cut into the rear wall near floor level to allow air to flow back into the house. Both slots are only sufficiently long to enter the annexe and wide enough so as not to inhibit air flow.

The rock-pile should be placed on a grating say about 30 cm above floor level, at about the same level as the top of the lower slot. The rocks are piled on to this to reach the lower edge of the upper slot and are insulated from the side walls by polyurethane batts or something similar to minimise the escape of heat to the exterior walls.

A fan, with the blades horizontal, is mounted above the rock-pile so as to pull air in through the upper slot and blow it down through the rock-pile. As a suggestion only, a Mistral Sunray fan type LD-12-10 could be suitable for this job. As the air blast from the fan is circular it seems appropriate to make the rock-pile circular and a rain water tank, with the top and bottom removed, has been suggested as a suitable container for the rocks which, of course, would also serve to keep the hot rocks away from contact with the outside walls of the annexe.

Consider a typical amateur orchid grower's glasshouse 16 feet × 9 feet with a height of 10 feet. In this example dimensions will be in feet and gallons as these are rather easier to visualise than metrics. The volume of the house is 1440 cubic feet and 8% of this is 115 cubic feet needed for the rock pile. A 750 gallon tank has a capacity of 120 cubic feet so would meet the 8% requirement. If the tank is 7 feet high this allows a space under it of 12 inches with 24 inches above for the fan, then the diameter of the tank will be about 4.7 feet, so the annexe needs to have a clear inside dimension of at least 5.5 feet to allow for any extra insulation. This gives a considerably greater volume than 15% of the glasshouse volume but this allowed for square packing of the rocks rather than circular packing into a round tank.

It is not the intention of this Topic to describe the construction of any form of glasshouse as this could take a complete book in itself, but simply to lay down some principles to follow when making the design.

Temperature

Heating
Australia is basically a sunny country and the disadvantages of a typical English type glasshouse for orchids has already been mentioned. The solar energy in winter in temperate N.S.W. is about five times greater than that in southern England. It is also of interest to note that leading orchid growers use glasshouses which have an appreciable height to allow orchids to be hung up near the roof and still allow room to walk underneath these.

Making the most effective use of winter sunlight has been detailed above in reference to the Solar Glasshouse. This is not necessarily the entire answer to the heating problem for we do at times have a week of rain when some additional heating is needed during the day as well as at night. All heating costs money

so it is good design if heat losses can be minimised. One useful method is double glazing which will reduce heat loss by some 30 to 35%. Lining the house with plastic sheeting or bubble plastic (UV light inhibited material is essential otherwise the lining will last a few weeks or months only). The bubble plastic is particularly good as the air space in the bubbles is fixed and air cannot move around due to convection currents. A heat saving factor of 40% is claimed for this bubble type plastic material. Lining the roof is especially important as the hot air accumulates here producing the greatest temperature differential with the outside air, hence greatest heat loss occurs here. A light duty fan is sometimes fitted in the upper part of the house to blow this hot air downwards where it can be more effective and cause less heat loss.

Unfortunately most commercial glasshouses have ventilators in the roof to let this hot air out in warm weather. In a house of your design place ventilators low down under benches and let cool air enter in summer and in the end and/or side walls near the top for the exit of hot air. Using blow-in and exhaust fans in lieu of some ventilators will be covered under 'Ventilation'.

The continued use of plastic lining in summer diffuses the direct sunlight and prevents plants from being burnt.

Heat is also lost via 'heat holes' in both the roof and around the walls. These occur where a metal glazing bar has one side exposed to the inner air and the other side to the outside air, which is usually the case. If you add up the area of these bars you will be surprised at just how large a heat hole exists in the glasshouse roof or walls. In the U.S.A. plastic covers are available to insulate the outside of these bars to minimise heat loss. Some glasshouses have the lower half of the door made of sheet metal which must be an excellent method of losing heat from the house.

By far the most efficient and clean method of heating is by electricity whether by a fan heater or by an off-peak hot water service. Installation is relatively simple, hence inexpensive, and control, whether by a simple thermostat or by some other integrated electronic control system, is quite straightforward.

The fan heater, when located at one end of the house (not the door end, designers note) a temperature gradient of about 2°C exists from the hot end to the cool end so allowing the discrete placement of genera. This type has the added advantage that air is circulated by the fan and does not become stagnant. The G.E. 3 kW model is generally sufficient for the modest amateur glasshouse of some 1500 cubic feet.

An off-peak hot water tank can be located in the house (so as not to lose any heat by leakage) and the hot water piped around under the benches, driven by a small pump which can be switched on and off by a thermostat or by a light sensitive device so that circulation is at night or dull days only. This type of system is satisfactory if you only want some warmth but it cannot be guaranteed to maintain the exact temperature you require at all times. It is valuable to give basic heat and any deficiency may be made up by a fan heater. In a mild climate, say in parts of Sydney, such a system will maintain about 13°C in a house of some 2000 cubic feet, most of the time.

Cooling
If the temperature of the glasshouse is to be kept under 30°C during our summers it is necessary to provide cooling. Simple glasshouses attempt to cool the air by opening ventilators but as 75% of the roof needs to be opened very few glasshouses can effectively cool by this method. Additionally if the outside air temperature is 35°C this method is not going to be very effective. Even heavy shading will not cool the hot dry winds.

The evaporation of water is the simplest and cheapest method of taking heat out of the air. This is dealt with under the chapter heading 'Substrates and Culture' so a few numerical examples will suffice here.

1. If the outside air temperature (OAT) is 35°C and the R.H. is 40% then the wet bulb reading would be 24°C. If this air is passed through an evaporative cooler and passed into the glasshouse the glasshouse temperature would theoretically be reduced to 24°C. In practice this is never quite attained and the actual temperature would be between 25 and 26°C.

2. If the OAT is 35°C and the R.H. 60% the wet bulb reading would be 28°C and if this air was passed into the house via an evaporative cooler the actual air temperature in the glasshouse would drop to just under the desirable upper limit of 30°C.

3. Hot dry winds often produce high temperatures, even on the coast. If the temperature is 39°C and R.H. 20% the wet bulb reading would be 22°C. By using an evaporative cooler the glasshouse air could be cooled to between 23 and 24°C. It is cooler in the glasshouse than it is outside.

4. Although the OAT may be 25°C the temperature inside the glasshouse on a sunny day is much higher. If the OAT is 25°C, the R.H. 70% the wet bulb temperature is 21°C. By using an evaporative cooler the glasshouse air could be cooled to 22 to 23°C. However satisfactory cooling to 25°C could be done simply by opening the door and all vents. The outside air is moist enough and no extra humidity is needed.

Therefore, an evaporative cooler can be thermostatically controlled to cut in, say with a glasshouse temperature of 27°C and rising. This will give the cooler, moist air introduced a chance to mix with the existing air, some of which will be exhausted through vents, possibly by an exhaust fan mounted in the top of the wall. The cooler air introduced near the floor will fill the glasshouse from the floor upwards.

Evaporative coolers can often be obtained secondhand or may be made by fitting a fan in front of an open mesh upon which water drips from a cistern of the self filling type.

Ventilation
Failure to seal the glasshouse properly will also result in heat loss but some growers contend that complete sealing is undesirable as this does inhibit air exchange between interior and exterior of the house. In this respect the following is of interest. When there is a difference in air pressure between the inside and outside due to temperature, wind or whatever a stream of air will flow through a hole in the house wall, say from outside to inside and will mix with the air inside the house. The air entering from a hole 1 cm in diameter will slow to 20% of its initial velocity when 20 cm inside the house and is by then very nearly (90%) mixed with the inside air. The incoming air fans out over a total solid angle of 22° and will be 8 cm wide at 20 cm from the hole.

A missing pane of glass say 40 cm square could feed in air for a distance of eight metres before becoming mixed with the house air and spread out over a width of 3 metres. This could subject a large number of plants to an unacceptably cold blast of air. This case would be typical of an open ventilator in winter.

In contrast the air flow from the house to an opening such as an exhaust fan is quite different in its action. The air flows from all directions at once and at a distance of one fan diameter from the fan inlet the air is moving at about 12% of the exit velocity.

The use of electric fans gives a better control of air movement than reliance on convection currents through ventilators although these latter, when correctly placed can also be useful. All air entering the glasshouse should be below bench level, either from blow-in fans or vents. All exhaust air should be via exhaust fans or vents high in the side or end walls. If the house is gabled an exhaust fan in the wall at the gable peak is useful. Fans ensure some air movement over the plants whereas convection currents may be negligible at times, and insufficient to move CO_2 depleted air away from the leaf area.

Humidity
This subject has been covered in the chapter on 'Substrates and Culture' but a few practical figures are given here.

For every 11°C (20°F) rise in glasshouse temperature (dry bulb) within the normal biological range the capacity of the air to hold water vapour doubles approximately and so (if no more is admitted) the relative humidity is reduced by half the previous value.

As an example if the amount of water vapour in the glasshouse air is 10 milligrams per gram of dry air and the air temperature is 25°C the R.H. = 52%. If the air temperature is now raised to 25 + 11 = 36°C the R.H. falls to half or about 26%. If the temperature is reduced by 11°C, i.e. 25 – 11 = 14°C the R.H. rises to 100% and condensation will occur, the water vapour will come out of the air and drip from the cold surfaces, e.g. outside windows.

The necessary amount of humidity may be obtained from a special device purchased as a Humidifier where almost invisible droplets are thrown into the air. Fine mist sprays may be installed in front of a fan to blow small water droplets into the air so that evaporation may take place or alternatively the floor may be kept moist several times a day in hot weather. The evaporation of water from here will maintain some degree of humidity.

Carbon dioxide enrichment
Very few amateur growers are able to instal CO_2 enrichment equipment but some do go as far as burning candles in the glasshouse or burning acetone via a wick. Once it was considered desirable to compost vegetable matter in the glasshouse to release CO_2 but this is seldom done now. However, water and fertiliser dripping on to a porous floor, such as the road-base suggested can promote bacterial growth with a consequent CO_2 enrichment of the air above the ground.

The normal CO_2 concentration in air is 0.032% or 320 parts per million which may rise to 600 ppm in industrial situations and is usually 10% higher in urban areas than in rural areas. One method of obtaining an increase in CO_2 in the glasshouse is for you to spend some time in there; also take your friends in to see your orchids. The normal human at rest exhales about 300 litres of air per hour and this contains about 5% CO_2 so an extra 15 litres of CO_2 in an hour is not to be dismissed lightly.

Normally the concentration of CO_2 in the glasshouse is falling all the time during the process of CO_2 fixation in the leaves whether this be by day or night (see Topic 4). Therefore, to maintain a reasonable level some replacement of air from outside is needed, hence ventilation of the house unless there is a CO_2 source inside the house.

Plants will normally respond to increased CO_2 levels by greater growth but to accomplish this a higher light intensity is required which may require additional lighting of a type which will promote photosynthesis, i.e. radiant energy at the appropriate wavelengths. See chapter on 'Substrates and Culture'.

Instrumentation
The following instruments are necessary in order to manage the glasshouse environment with any degree of skill.
Maximum/Minimum thermometer. This is a reasonably cheap dual scale thermometer which can be reset every day, every week or whatever and will indicate the maximum and minimum temperatures in the house since the last re-set. The latest types are re-set by pushing a button rendering the previously used small magnets unnecessary.
Wet and Dry Bulb thermometer. This is a dual thermometer mounted on a base board together with a scale. The wet bulb is fitted with a wick which dips into a water container and so keeps one bulb cooler than the other providing the humidity is

not 100% or the water has not been used up and the container not re-filled. Take two readings from the thermometer scales and refer to the table, usually fixed to the instrument, to obtain the relative humidity.

Inside/Outside thermometer. This is valuable in determining the efficacy of the glasshouse cooling system and its use is obvious.

TOPIC 2. IMPORTING ORCHIDS & PLANT QUARANTINE

It is not difficult to import orchid plants either fully grown or as small plants in flasks. These latter are already growing under sterile conditions and should be free from fungal or bacterial contamination when supplied to the purchaser. However, many growers prefer to import mature plants and although the procedures are more complex they are not at all difficult. A few nurseries in Australia advertise as being agents for orchid plant suppliers in other countries and it is only necessary to make your selection from the available catalogue, pay your money and sit back and wait.

If you prefer to go it alone then the following information will prove invaluable. The first problem is to decide whether you want to import species or hybrids. If importing species it is much less costly to obtain these from their country of origin, e.g. Philippine orchids from the Philippines and not from a supplier in some other country who has already gone to some expense to obtain these plants from their origin, hence each plant is more costly. Many overseas nurseries exporting orchids advertise in Journals such as the American Orchid Society Bulletin and the Orchid Digest. Copies of these are usually available from the library of your local Orchid Society. Send for a catalogue or list from the most likely supplier of your needs and make a selection. Avoid ordering expensive 'special selection' plants until you have had some experience both with the supplier and the quarantine aspects of importing. The next move is to co-operate with the local plant quarantine inspector or office. Ask for a Form QP36, complete this and return it to the quarantine office. The form asks questions like these:

1. The nature and number of plants for which a permit is desired? Usually the term 'orchids' is sufficient to describe the plants. Although you may order certain species some substitution may be necessary. Also state a range for the number (e.g. 25 to 30). If you order 25 a few 'free' plants may be placed into the box.

2. Documents likely to accompany plants? These are usually:
(a) a list of plants supplied
(b) a Phytosanitary Certificate from the Quarantine Department of country of origin.

3. How are the plants to be despatched? This is usually air-freight preferably by our own flag carrier for ease of handling this end but other countries tend to favour their own flag carriers. At Sydney airport, for example, Plant Quarantine have an office in the Qantas freight building. Ask about this before placing your order.

4. When are the plants expected to arrive in Australia? Be generous about this. Allow two weeks for your import approval to be returned, ten days for your airmail order to reach the supplier, seven days for the supplier to deal with the order and one or two days to air-freight the package. Usually one day from

South East Asia and two days for further afield if there is a direct air link between the country of export and an Australian city. Transhipping within Australia from the first airport to other places may take a day or two.

Orders from places without a direct air link are anyone's guess, e.g. Peru, where transhipping once or twice may be needed.

5. Where are the plants to be quarantined? This can be either at the Government quarantine station in the State or in an approved private quarantine house. These latter may have a yearly import quota so it is necessary to check with the owner prior to completing the form.

After approval one copy of the QP36 now bearing an approval number will be returned to you. Send off your order asking the supplier to address the package to

Plant Quarantine Office at . . . . Airport for (your own name and phone number)

The package must also be marked clearly with your import permit number, e.g. 82/QP36/—/—. States may differ on this so check with your own Quarantine Office.

Ask the supplier to pay the airfreight which you can encourage by adding to your bank draft 50% of the value of the orchids ordered unless you can determine the exact cost of the airfreight. Without knowing the size and weight of the package this can be difficult. Some nurseries ask that 33% of the value of the orchids be added but this is usually not sufficient if the plants are a 'good buy'. Any reputable nursery will return any amount received in excess of the actual costs.

Unless the air-freight is pre-paid the plants will not be released to quarantine which may precipitate a hurried and inconvenient trip to the airport. As orchid plants are not heavy, the air-freight costs are based on the size of the carton, rather than on its weight. A volume of 7000 cubic centimetres or 427 cubic inches is regarded as 1 kilogramme and charged as such. However, there is a minimum charge, usually equivalent to 5 kilogrammes.

The costing (1982) from a few overseas airports is shown, purely as a guide. It is advisable to check with your local airport office before sending off the order, particularly if transhipping within Australia is needed.

Manila to Sydney: per kg = A$4.70 minimum charge = A$27.00
Bangkok to Sydney: per kg = A$5.75 minimum charge = A$28.20
Taipei to Sydney: per kg = A$5.75 minimum charge = A$28.25
Hawaii to Sydney: per lb = A$3.00 minimum charge = A$37.20
Note that for some unknown reason freight ex Hawaii is given in pounds weight rather than kg.

If you are going overseas and intend to bring plants back with you the procedure is much the same. Complete the paper work prior to departure and obtain an approval number and the QP36. Airline clerks at overseas passenger counters sometimes refuse to accept cartons of live plants as passenger luggage on the grounds that people cannot take live plant material into Australia. This is what they have been told and they take some convincing that this is not correct. Waving a QP36 in front of them does help.

It is possible to arrive at the Australian airport with a carton of orchids and without a QP36 and have these accepted at the Customs counter and sent to a nominated plant quarantine by the plant inspector on duty. He will give you a receipt for them and send them into the quarantine centre for fumigation. However, it is better to come armed with an import permit the number of which can be marked on the carton.

The number of orchids which you intend to import cannot always be stated with any accuracy prior to departure so make sure you ask for a large enough number, say 100. The local markets at some places, e.g. Bangkok, are a good source of material and not to be passed up because your stated quota was not large enough. The amount which you can bring back depends on how much you can get through as passenger's luggage or are prepared to pay as excess baggage. Orchids are reasonably light in weight.

Remember no soil at all can be imported and must be washed off the roots prior to packing if any has been used. Some orchids are sold in small clay pots holding broken crocks. These are not only heavy but if they break or become loose in transit they tend to cut the plant unnecessarily, so remove the pots and crocks as much as possible and discard. Plants in wooden slat baskets are satisfactory but the wooden baskets should be tied firmly to the carton. It is useful to have 'twisties' for this purpose. Take with you some of the metal type plant labels and wire ties. Anything less robust usually suffers over the period of quarantine so one may be left with a collection of nameless plants. In any case do not trust nursery labels. Attach your own metal tag giving each plant a code number and list these in duplicate, one copy for the carton and one for you.

A useful numbering system is made up from the first three letters of your name, the plant number (say, commencing from 100) and three letters identifying the source.

For example   MOR 106 SEL

Such a code allows the ready identification of your plants on the quarantine bench, it allows you to check that all plants have been accounted for and finally, when they flower and identification is sought, the origin of the material is available and no guess-work or memory is needed.

If the carton of plants is too large for the passenger cabin it will have to go with the luggage. It is helpful to label the carton in large red lettering 'Live plants—keep warm'. Hopefully the plants will then be stowed in an appropriate place on the aircraft.

Quarantine charges. At the time of writing these are:
Initial examination and fumigation in gas chamber of methyl bromide.
Consignment not exceeding 25 plants: $8.00
Consignment exceeding 25 plants: $13.40 plus 25 cents per plant in excess of 25.
Care of plants in quarantine nursery (Government): $25 plus 40 cents per plant.
Private quarantine houses have various rates which should be settled at the time of negotiation for services. Orchids remain in quarantine for a minimum of three months or until such time as the inspector is satisfied that they are free from disease.

In general terms one can buy the plants at their country of origin, pay the airfreight and quarantine charges at a cost of about half the price of the plants in Australia, if they are available. This applies to species only as many hybrids are sold at quite high prices if they have won awards. Naturally it does not pay to import less than say 25 plants as the airfreight becomes a major item. Also many nurseries will not handle orders less than US$30 or US$50. United States dollars is the usual currency used by orchid nurseries and the bank draft should be made out in this currency.

In some ways Australia is fortunate. As an island continent we are isolated from the rest of the world and better control can be exercised over the importation of plant and animal products. With the rapid transit of people by air, plants can be in their country of origin one day and in Australia the next.

In a country so dependent on primary production from the land it is essential that plant diseases and pests be kept out as far as possible so do not try to smuggle plants through Customs, even if they are only orchids. Experience has shown that imported pests are often more injurious here than in their own country of origin. The predators which naturally keep them in check are usually not here, a whole range of new host plants is available for their support and they spread far and wide before we are aware of their existence here.

Diseases such as the plague and cholera necessitated people-quarantine in the early 1400s but plant quarantine did not come into effect until the early 1900s. Australia commenced plant quarantine in 1909, the Commonwealth Department of Health being the responsible organisation. However the State Department of Agriculture, Division of Horticulture, carried out the work of inspection of imported plant material.

TOPIC 3.
MYCORRHIZAL ASSOCIATIONS

The first observation that fungal growth was present in orchid roots was noted in the early part of the 19th century but it was then regarded as parasitic growth. Towards the end of the 19th century the nature of the fungal growth was recognised as contributing to the food supply of the plant. Between 1903 and 1909 Noel Bernard, in a series of experiments, showed that the presence of endotrophic mycelium was essential for the germination of orchid seed and the initial growth of the seedling. Endotrophic mycelium is a fungal strand which grows within the plant as opposed to ectotrophic mycelium present on many plants and which covers the root or tuber externally but does not enter it. Bernard was able to grow orchid seedlings to a suitable size for transplanting in the absence of fungus if sugar was supplied. Bernard was French and his work preceded that of Knudson, who is well known for his application of sugar to nutrient culture gels (see Chapter 9).

There are two different types of endotrophic mycelium relevant to the orchid plant. These are:

1. Tolypophagy where the fungal coils of the mycelium enter the roots and are there killed and digested by the plant.
2. Ptyophagy where only the tip of the fungus enters the digestive cells of the orchid (although it grows in the outer cells) and the contents of the fungal mycelia are squirted into the digestive cells.

This type of fungus-plant relationship is called a mycorrhizal association, not exclusive to orchids but present in many plants. However, the essentiality of this association is slightly different when applied to orchids so the use of the term 'mycorrhizal', which means root fungus may seem mis-applied.

Many non-orchid plants germinate in the normal manner and are only dependent on the mycorrhizal association for continued living or at least for good growth. Only a few plants have no such associations and these include the sedge family (Cyperaceae) and the mustard family (Brassicaceae). Contrary to general opinion, tropical soils are of very poor nutritive quality, most of the available nutrients being held in the living plants or in their leaf and stem litter. This layer of litter is useless to the plant and needs to be decomposed, an action undertaken by fungi. It seems a much more efficient transfer scheme if the decomposition products can be transferred by the fungus directly into the plant rather than to the soil and then have to be taken up by whatever plant roots are present at the decomposition site. The transfer of phosphorus direct from the fungus to plant is an example, not only of nutritional efficiency but as a method of conserving this scarce element which, if it entered the soil as an anion, could well be leached downwards or into streams by the heavy rainfall. It has been estimated that almost the entire useable fertility of tropical rain forest soil is in the fungal mycelia which inhabit it, rather than in the soil proper.

The orchid seed is different from most seeds in that the only reserve food supply is contained in a few minute droplets of oil, whereas most seeds have an endosperm which constitutes a large food reserve to be used during germination. In the orchid the oil droplets are used up very early in the germination process so the seed dies unless it has an externally supplied food pipeline. This is the so-called mycorrhizal association, not with a root but with a seed which is not even a differentiated embryo. In most seeds the embryo is formed into root, stem and leaf tissue ready to grow upon demand, but the proto-embryo of the orchid consists only of a few cells which hopefully will differentiate into root and leaf.

The fungus enters the seed through the suspensor, a short tail at one end of the proto-embryo. Is the fungus on a good-will mission or is it just looking for food and finds the proto-embryo a satisfactory source? The latter seems more likely as if fungal growth is uncontrolled the fungus will kill the seed or seedling. If the orchid seed kills the fungus, it is itself doomed, so there needs to be a mutual truce between the two, to live and let live but no doubt, this sometimes gets out of hand to the detriment of the orchid.

The adult orchid plant has no real need for fungal association, particularly when fed in culture, if it can photosynthesise. Presumably when growing on trees or in the ground in nature there is such an association which proves useful to the orchid. Whether the fungus receives carbohydrates or other useful nutrients from the plant in return for inorganic nutrients seems hard to discover or perhaps no one has tried very hard. The fungal mycelium consists of protein, carbohydrates and oil so when this is digested by the orchid more than just inorganic nutrients are obtained.

The growth of saprophytic orchids is quite another matter. These contain very little or no chlorophyll and are dependent on the mycorrhizal association for nutrition. In this case it is a true endotrophic mycorrhizal association as the fungus penetrates the root system. In the geophytic orchids with small tubers, these latter are not penetrated beyond the epidermis, the fungus being kept at bay by chemicals generated within the tuber. These control the fungal growth and prevent death of the orchid but the new roots re-generated every growing season must be re-infected by the fungus.

Epiphytic orchids may have either roots hanging free in air or roots attached to bark or similar substrate. Infection by fungi is largely restricted to the latter type, the former being free from infection.

Fungi belong to a kingdom of their own as fungal nutrition and reproduction are very different from plants. Additionally most fungi have an imperfect stage which is purely vegetative (i.e. no fruiting bodies) and the various genera and species can be extremely difficult to identify or even classify until the perfect or fruiting stage is seen. Some effort and ingenuity has often to be expended in encouraging a fungus to fruit so that it can be correctly classified by fungal taxonomists.

This has caused a lot of confusion and difficulty in the classification of orchid mycorrhizal fungi the imperfect stages of which are placed in a broad barrel labelled *Rhizoctonia*, a genus also responsible for plant disease. Various fungal isolates from green leaved orchids have been judged to be species of *Rhizoctonia* but saprophytes devoid of or sparsely furnished with chlorophyll are associated with another type of fungus, hence are unlikely to grow in 'a pot of orchid compost' inhabited only with *Rhizoctonia*. However, the whole question is still rather clouded, resolution of the problem is slow and difficult.

Within these broad limits it is not of vital concern to the orchid grower which fungi form the mycorrhiza of which orchids. However, the saprophytes seem to have developed a close association with a white wood rotting fungus present in some trees, hence it is impracticable to culture these orchids outside of their natural habitat.

Chapter 1 dealt briefly with orchid seed distribution and possible fungal distribution. In respect of Krakatao Island, geophytes were the first orchids to migrate. Just how these became associated with the correct fungus is a matter of conjecture but one may reasonably suppose that the fungi would firstly re-grow in the soil rather than on tree branches. When these latter became infested with fungus the epiphytic seeds could germinate and populate them.

Not all forest trees support orchid growth. Adjacent trees with crossing branches may have one tree devoid of orchid plants while the other is covered. Some barks are known to exude phenolic substances like tannic, ellagic and gallic acids. It has been postulated that these are toxic to the orchid seed. However, it seems more likely that such phenolic substances are inhibitory to the growth of fungi which is now no longer present to penetrate the seed, no matter how much of this is deposited on the tree bark. Experimental work does not appear to have been done on this aspect but it is known that substances such as Caffeic acid, (3.4. di-hydroxy cinnamic acid) a phenolic acid, can inhibit the growth of some plant disease fungi by being supplied from the plant itself.

The fact that orchids do grow and flourish in nature indicates that there is a balance between the fungus killing the orchid and the orchid killing the fungus so that both may live in close association.

Many plants produce protective chemicals called collectively, phytoalexins, a name coined to indicate plant origin and activity in warding off attack. Phytoalexins have been found in tuberous rooted orchids and named as Orchinol, Loroglossol and Hircinol. There are three-ring phenanthrene type structures rather than the simpler phenolic type. The tubers of *Orchis militaris* begin to produce Orchinol 36 hours after infection by the fungus and this reaches a maximum production rate in seven days. As the fungus penetrates the orchid tissue the concentration of Orchinol in that area increases so preventing a 'run-away' growth of the fungus.

TOPIC 4.   CARBON FIXATION

The latter part of Chapter 6 on Substrates and Culture forms an introduction to this Topic. In earlier chapters of this book frequent reference was made to carbon dioxide and its importance to plant growth. Carbon dioxide (CO_2) exists in the atmosphere near the earth's surface at an average concentration of 0.032% or 320 parts per million (ppm). However, it is of little use to the plant as a gas or even in solution, somehow it must be incorporated into a substance within the plant. This is carbon fixation and this Topic will attempt to show the various methods of carbon fixation known to exist in plants and then refer this to specific orchids.

On planet Earth carbon has a prime position where it plays a leading role in living organisms of all types, by providing a chemical skeleton upon which all the other useful elements may hang. This role is largely because of the ability of carbon to join, without limit, to itself by an electrostatic bonding system so building up large molecules from very simple ones.

As examples, here is carbon bonded in a long chain form, such as encountered in fats and waxes, chlorophyll and many other substances and in a ring form such as in some flower colouring compounds.

```
                            C
                          /   \
             C          C       C
             |          |       |
 — C — C — C — C — C — C         C
         |              |       |
         C              C       C
                          \   /
                            C
```

The short lines representing the electrostatic bonding between carbon atoms.

As well as this property it also bonds readily to other elements in nature such as hydrogen, oxygen, phosphorus and sulphur. As an example:

```
       H   H        O
       |   |       //
 H —  C — C  — C
       |   |       \
       H   H        OH
              or
              H
              |
              C
            /   \\
   HO —  C        C — H
          ||       |
   H —  C         C = S
            \   /
              O
```

in the ring compound the C ring has been broken to include an oxygen which is quite a common occurrence. The double lines indicate a double bond between the atoms, shown here only for the purpose of being correct.

Carbon is not the only element which bonds extensively to itself; silicon is another and who knows by what means or for what reasons we were saved from such a gritty fate. Inhabitants of far off planets may have evolved from silicon and derive their sustenance from rocks rather than from a black amorphous substance like carbon!

All of these atoms do not join together of their own volition, but like most things, they require energy. Energy on its own accomplishes much but to accomplish it at low temperatures is quite another matter and if living organisms are going to continue to live, the temperatures must be restricted within the biological limits.

All life from the simplest bacterium to the most complex mammal, has evolved a set of proteins to bring about chemical reactions within minimum temperatures and modest expenditure of energy. These special proteins are called enzymes and any consideration of carbon fixation needs to acknowledge the existence of these and the part they play in the process. The nature of the enzymes is determined by the genetic code locked away in the chromosomes. In fact, that is really all the genetic code does, determine the enzymes, which then determine the nature of the organism be it a bacterium, plant or mammal. One often hears about 'the gene for blue eyes' or 'the gene for blue flowers'. Such a gene does not exist, only the genes to make the enzymes which in turn are capable, if not otherwise interfered with, of making the substance for blue eyes or blue flowers.

So the enzymes are made in the plant and then in turn make all of the other complex compounds used for growth but what of the energy required to carry out these processes? Ultimately all energy for life comes from the sun either directly, as for plants, or indirectly by ingestion of plant food by other organisms (except for a few bacteria). The green plant by virtue of a pigment called chlorophyll is capable of absorbing energy from visible light and storing this in a chemical bond of a phosphorus compound.

So important is this light absorbing process that it needs some explanation before proceeding to carbon fixation. Photosynthesis is a term introduced when only the general overall principle of the need for light was understood. We now have a better understanding of the processes involved and the 'photo' part is largely quite distinct from the 'synthesis' part. At one stage these two processes were referred to as the 'light and dark reactions', terms which may appear in older texts but which have now fallen into disuse. However, the term photosynthesis is still widely used as a general umbrella term meaning everything and anything which occurs to give the green plant its autotrophic existence.

The photosynthetic site is a small body called a chloroplast (an organelle) some 5 to 8 micrometres $\times$ 1 micrometre (see Appendix 2) and some 50 to 150 are present in each plant cell, being embedded in a protein sap and free to move therein. Each chloroplast has a complex structure which will not be elaborated on here as it is not essential to the understanding of carbon fixation. The chloroplast contains a pigment called chlorophyll which has energy absorbing properties (because of its chemical structure) in the general red and blue areas of the visible spectrum and it reflects green light which is why leaves appear green whereas, in the dark they are not green at all!

About 10 forms of chlorophyll are known, types a and b being the most common. Two other pigments are present in leaves, carotenes and xanthophylls both appearing to be yellow and it is these pigments which show through if chlorophyll is destroyed, such as by placing orchid plants in full summer sunlight.

The chloroplast is not just a passive organelle, it is capable of self replication and production of its own distinctive proteins. One theory is that in the distant past, some 1800 megayears ago, the photosynthetic cyanobacteria (blue-green algae) entered non-photosynthesising organisms, formed a relationship of benefit to both organisms and so was the forerunner of our present plants. (Another fascinating side issue which must be left aside here as it is not relevant to carbon fixation in present day plants.)

In the green plant photosynthesis is carried out by two reactions initiated by light in the blue and red parts of the spectrum. The details of these reactions are lengthy and not significant to this Topic except that in one system water is split to provide hydrogen ions and electrons, so we have—

$$2H_2O \rightarrow 4H^+ + O_2 + 4 \text{ electrons}$$

This process uses both manganese and chlorine, both elements being essential, in small amounts, for successful plant growth.

The electrons are driven 'uphill' against a potential gradient by the energy derived from light exciting chlorophyll. They are then free to roll 'downhill' giving up energy as they do so. This energy is stored in a phosphorus compound Adenosine Triphosphate (ATP) and can be used as the energy source for carbon fixation. It is of interest to note that this substance ATP is universal on earth as an energy storage bin in all living organisms even the non-photosynthetic ones wherein the energy comes from degradation of fats and sugars. This universality of ATP says a lot for the common origin of all life.

The hydrogen ions which are so necessary to join with the carbon atoms to make up sugars, proteins, cellulose, anthocyanins for flower colour and many other substances like nectar and pollen are then derived from water as shown above. Hydogen ions are not permitted to wander free about the plant but are joined to another phosphorus containing compound called Nicotinamide Adenine Dinucleotide Phosphate (NADP) where they are stored until required.

So to summarise, light energy is absorbed by chlorophyll, converted to chemical energy and transferred to a storage bin called ATP. Water is split and hydrogen is stored in another bin called NADP. In this process the elements chlorine, manganese and phosphorus are used. Oxygen is given off as a gas surplus to requirements. This evolution of oxygen gives some support to the view often expressed that it gives one a 'lift' to relax in a garden on a sunny day.

From this point on, chlorophyll ceases to have any significance although the reactions of carbon fixation occur in the chloroplast. The resulting products are then processed by the other parts of the cell.

There are three different forms of carbon fixation known at present. These are:

1. The C$_3$ type, sometimes called the Calvin cycle after Calvin, Benson and Bassham, the principals of the team who in 1949 at the University of California, worked out the first carbon fixation pattern.

2. The C$_4$ type sometimes called the Hatch-Slack pathway after the two Australian plant physiologists who elucidated this pathway.

3. The CAM type, short for Crassulacean Acid Metabolism, because it was first discovered in plants of the Crassulaceae. If more plant physiologists worked with orchids it may well have been called Orchidacean Acid Metabolism or OAM. It is a variation of the C$_4$ pathway and is most important in orchid culture.

The C$_3$ pathway occurs in most of our temperate region garden plants and is also applicable to many orchids. However, with 20 000 species of orchids it is hardly likely that the pathway for each one will be known for a long time so we must use the general characteristics of a plant to forecast the type of carbon fixation pathway it may possess.

The C$_4$ pathway is typical of tropical grasses including maize and sugar cane. Surprisingly bamboo is a C$_3$ plant as are the more temperate grasses of wheat and oats. One feature of C$_4$ plants is their ability to assimilate rapidly CO$_2$ and so give increased production at high ambient temperatures. Grass leaves

can receive effective illumination from both sides without their photosynthetic mechanisms becoming light saturated in full tropical sun. If C$_3$ plants are mixed with C$_4$ grasses on a sunny tropical hillside the C$_4$ grasses will soon dominate the situation.

Only one orchid is known to be of the C$_4$ pattern in its young leaves and this is *Arundina graminifolia*, the specific epithet meaning grass leaved. Readers may remember meeting this orchid in the Ecology section of Chapter 1 as a 'weed' orchid which, along with grasses, colonised cleared hillsides in Malaysia. This C$_4$ property of its young leaves would most certainly give it an even chance against the competition from C$_4$ grasses until the orchid became high enough to receive its share of light in the ecological competition. The older leaves then revert to the C$_3$ method of fixation but why this occurs remains something of a mystery.

CAM type of carbon fixation occurs in plants which generally may suffer water stress. Typical of these are the cacti and succulents such as *Agave, Opuntia, Aloe* and *Crassula*. Many epiphytic orchids can fall into this water stress category, particularly those growing in tree tops where rainfall is seasonal. Orchid genera having species with CAM characteristics are *Aerides, Arachnis, Ascocentrum, Phalaenopsis, Laelia, Epidendrum, Bulbophyllum, Dendrobium* and *Coelogyne*. Not all species in the genera are CAM, some have been shown to be C$_3$, others have not been tested.

There is also the question whether CAM characteristics are modified to any extent by environment, purely as a temporary measure and not a genetic change. In other words is the ability to fix carbon by both the CAM method and the C$_3$ method present in the plant at all times, the most suitable one being used to meet the environment.

Earlier in this Topic the importance and function of enzymes was mentioned briefly. As may be expected enzymes are of paramount importance in the fixing of carbon into usable substances. Enzymes are named in accordance with their function, the name ending in -ase, e.g. oxidase is involved in oxidation, carboxylase joins CO$_2$ to another substance. One enzyme of particular importance in carbon fixation in all plants is Ribulose diphosphate carboxylase. This is not only important but very abundant, probably the most abundant in nature, about 1/4 to 1/8 of the total leaf protein is formed by this enzyme. It is so named because it joins the 5-carbon sugar Ribulose diphosphate (RuDP) to CO$_2$ to form an unstable 6-carbon compound which promptly breaks up into 3-carbon compounds called phosphoglyceric acid (PGA). This is shown by the formula:

$$
\begin{array}{ccccc}
& H & H & & O \\
& | & | & & \diagup\!\!\diagup \\
H - & C - & C - & C & \\
& | & | & & \diagdown \\
H_2PO_3 - & O & OH & & OH
\end{array}
$$

where the three carbons are clearly shown. We see here the first clue why some plants are called C$_3$, the first recognisable product from carbon fixation is a 3-carbon substance.

As a side issue the metallic ion of magnesium is vital for the proper operation of RuDP carboxylase. It is well recognised that magnesium is a constituent of chlorophyll but only a small percentage is needed for this role; much more is required as an enzyme activator, particularly of RuDP carboxylase due to the large amount of this substance present; yet this role of magnesium seldom rates a mention.

The PGA so formed is converted to other carbon compounds, part of it being recycled to form RuDP so that the carbon fixation process may continue. The remainder is used to form sugars and subsequently other necessary compounds for growth or stored as starch, an insoluble combination of the sugar glucose, to be put back into solution and carried around the plant as it is needed, frequently during the hours of darkness.

From the above we would expect that in C_4 plants, the first substance formed in the carbon fixation process would be a four carbon substance. This is so; the substance is a four-carbon acid called oxaloacetic acid which quickly disappears being converted to another more stable 4-carbon acid, malic acid. It takes about 7 seconds for the CO_2 absorbed to become malic acid.

If a 4-carbon substance is formed by adding CO_2 we would expect to commence with a 3-carbon substance and this is so. It is another phosphorus containing 3-carbon compound called Phosphoenol pyruvic acid (PEP) and the enzyme is again, as expected, PEP carboxylase. The leaf cells adjacent to the leaf surface are the first to receive CO_2 and in C_4 plants the mechanism to convert this to malic acid is found here.

The malic acid so formed must be processed in some way to be useful to the plant and C_4 plants have a further factory stowed away inside the leaf towards its centre when looking at the leaf edge on. This inner processing factory receives the malic acid from the external cells and decarboxylates it, i.e. the CO_2 is removed and this is then processed in the normal way via the Calvin cycle, as in C_3 plants, sugars and starches being formed for future use. Measurements have shown that C_4 plants, e.g. maize, have about 3 to 7 times the photosynthetic rate of temperate zone trees and shrubs which are solely C_3 plants.

In C_4 plants there is a division of labour among the cells of the leaf but this division of labour means more workers which means more energy is used from the ATP storage bin, so what makes the C_4 pathway plants so much more efficient in their operation than C_3 plants?

To examine this question we must consider respiration, that is the use by the plant cell organelles (of which there are many not mentioned in this text) of reserve food, e.g. sugars. Respiration is a continuous process in all living organisms at normal biological temperatures. One waste product of respiration is CO_2 in plants as in animals. When a plant is working at food production, i.e. photosynthesis, its respiration rate goes up just as when animal muscles are being activated the respiration rate increases. In plants this increased work during daylight hours is called photorespiration and in C_3 plants it can be 2 to 3 times greater than the respiration rate during darkness. In C_3 plants in light, respiration is taking place in all cells containing chloroplasts and much of the CO_2 evolved escaped from the leaf. It is not captured by RuDP carboxylase because this also has an affinity for oxygen which competes with the CO_2 for the services of the enzyme and the enzyme is not able to assimilate the excess CO_2.

In C_4 plants it is only the inner factory of cells which show evidence of photorespiration, the respiration rate of the outer cells responsible for capturing the CO_2 initially and adding it to PEP, is not affected by light. Any CO_2 released from the inner cells is recaptured by the outer cells before it escapes and is re-used.

One may think if photorespiration occurs in light, then perhaps the higher the light intensity the harder the plant is working, so the photorespiration rate will increase. This is so in C_3 species and this is then processed in the normal more photosynthesis. Light saturation is reached. In C_4 plants photorespiration is not a problem so these plants can use higher light intensities at high temperature and are ideally suited to growing in open land sunblazing tropical conditions.

The process is somewhat more complex than this but the above explanation is sufficient for the reader to follow the elements of carbon fixation.

Although only two orchids are known so far to have a C_4 structure and capability some time was spent on this pathway because it is relevant to CAM plants of which there are many in the orchid flora.

It was mentioned earlier that the CAM type of carbon fixation had developed in plants which are subject to water stress. The C_3 and C_4 plants which actively absorb CO_2 in daylight, need to have the leaf stomates wide open for CO_2 entry. This invariably leads to water loss from the leaf, a process called transpiration, and one which is not entirely a loss as it produces nutrient movement through the plant and also into the root zone where such nutrients can be taken up into the plant.

For plants already subject to water stress what better way of conserving water is there than to close the stomates during daylight hours when it is hot and the humidity is low, and open the stomates at night when it is cool and the humidity is high. (The Ecology notes of Chapter 1 mention the rain and cloud cover in the tropics just before sunset, which cools the air and increases humidity.) This is the action of CAM plants. The stomates open at night and absorb CO_2 and combine this with PEP to produce malic acid just like the C_4 plants but there is a difference.

This malic acid is stored in the cell vacuole, a cavity in the cell used for storing nutrients in a water solution (**Fig. 5-1**), something which could not be done in a proteinaceous cytoplasm. Storage is necessary because the remainder of the action is processed by RuDP carboxylase which is activated by light. When daylight occurs the stomates close and the malic acid breaks up into PEP and CO_2, the latter entering the C_3 Calvin cycle and sugars produced.

To summarise, both CAM plants and C_4 plants use both PEP carboxylase and RuDP carboxylase to fix and process CO_2. In C_4 plants the two actions are separated in space in the leaf. In CAM plants the two actions occur in the same plant cell, but are separated in time, photorespiration is also absent.

This then is a plant adaption, genetically determined but controlled by the environment and promoted by hot, dry conditions. It is worth noting that the CAM type of fixation at night by epiphytic orchids in the tree tops occurs when the stomates of the tree leaves are closed and not expressing any interest in CO_2 absorption leaving it all for the orchids and bromeliads which are also epiphytic CAM plants.

It has been observed that some CAM plants under a wet environmental influence, switch to partial C_3 type carbon fixation, the stomates remaining open during the early morning hours of daylight. Whether this is applicable to orchids is not known at this stage. When growing CAM plants in the glasshouse it is advisable to ensure good ventilation at night so that the CO_2 is plentiful if it is needed.

Earlier in this Topic it was mentioned that with 20 000 species of orchids the investigation of the carbon fixation pathway for each one may not be known for a long time (or ever) so the general characteristics of the plant must serve as an indication of the possible pathway.

As a general guide all thick leaved orchids, almost a succulent type of leaf, should be considered a likely candidate for CAM. This may apply to some geophytes which are known to grow in very dry sandy conditions, almost in a desert micro-climate. Some of the genera in which CAM species are known to exist were given earlier in this Topic.

Typical C_4 plants are those which grow in open spaces in full tropical sun. Apart from *Arundina* some *Arachnis* species which require full sunlight and some terete leaf *Vanda* species may have a C_4 tendency.

C_3 plants are typically thin leaved and grow in places where the available water is ample and not a limiting factor. *Coelogyne massangeana* with its large thin plicate leaves is a C_3 plant. Not much work has been done on the *Oncidium* but *O. flexuosum* and *O. lanceanum* are known to be C_3. Probably some of the thicker leaved species, such as *O. cavendishianum* are CAM plants.

TOPIC 5.   ORCHID TAXONOMY & NOMENCLATURE

The two words 'Taxonomy and Nomenclature' in the title have been used deliberately. Very often the single word Taxonomy is used, quite incorrectly, to indicate or refer to the naming of plants. Taxonomy is the recognition of the identity of a plant and the systematic classification of it at any level. For example, to recognise the identity of a plant as an orchid places it (at a high level) within the Orchidaceae. It has been classified, the high level referring to the classification at family level, it seldom being necessary to go higher into the Order or Class. Taxon (pl. Taxa) is a general term applicable to any taxonomic element irrespective of classification level. The following levels, taken individually, are all Taxa; Family, Tribe, Genus, Species.

Nomenclature is the science of naming things, in this case, plants. There are certain rules to follow in order that the name shall be valid. Any name not valid is illegitimate and not recognisable botanically.

So having determined that the plant is an orchid, i.e. within the taxon Orchidaceae, further classification may place it within the taxon Vandeae (Tribe) and then within the taxon Sarcanthinae (Sub-tribe) and then within the taxon *Arachnis* (Genus) and so on. If comprehensive and exhaustive research indicates that the plant cannot be classified into an existing taxon then the taxonomist may give it a name and describe the plant in accordance with an international set of rules. This is nomenclature.

Giving a plant a name is a risky business unless one has a very comprehensive library and herbarium at one's disposal. In fact it is usual to consult the content of several herbaria throughout the world to be sure that the plant has not been described previously and this is often a lengthy process. The extensive range of orchids throughout the world and the very large number of species has made it desirable for some botanists to specialise in orchid plants from a given geographical area.

There is a general tendency at times for persons other than herbarium taxonomists to classify plants ostensibly new to science. These classifications are not always validly published in accordance with international rules. Even if validly published the classifications are not always recognised by all taxonomists throughout the world. Acceptance is usually a matter of 'wait and see'. If other taxonomists increasingly adopt the new classification and nomenclature it is regarded as accepted and becomes 'law'. It would not serve any useful purpose here to review all of the Rules governing nomenclature. These are set down in the International Code of Botanical Nomenclature which is revised from time to time.

It is sufficient to say that there are two important rules.
1. The name and description (a diagnosis in Botanical Latin) of the plant must be validly published and the type specimen cited along with the name of the herbarium in which it has been deposited for scrupulous preservation. 'Validly published' means published in a recognised Journal of botanical substance. This covers a wide range of documents but specifically excludes tradesmen's catalogues, newspapers and similar 'for-the-public' magazines.
2. The rule of priority of names must be applied. If it can be shown that an orchid was given a name in 1888 and another name given to the same species in 1889, then the latter name is illegitimate even though the plant has been known by this name for many years. The earlier name must be applied to the plant and take priority. Names given prior to 1753 when Linnaeus

published his 'Species Plantarum' are not considered as having priority as there must be some commencing point in history.

This rule accounts for some of the otherwise inexplicable name changes which occur from time to time. An example of this appears in Botanical Museum Leaflets from Harvard University Vol. 23 No. 4 of June 30 1972 wherein Leslie A. Garay explains why *Sarcanthus* (1826) is illegitimate and *Cleisostoma* (1825) is its replacement name.

Occasionally we see a case of *Nomen conservandum* (nom.cons.) i.e. a name conserved for use regardless of priority. These names are preferably such as have come into general use in the 50 years following their publication or which have been used in monographs and important floristic works up to 1890. There are some 40 *Nomina generica conservanda* in the Orchidaceae including such well known genera as *Bulbophyllum, Calanthe, Miltonia, Dendrobium* and *Pterostylis.*

This system is not to be confused with the so-called 'Horticultural Equivalents' given in the Handbook of Orchid Nomenclature and Registration. This list of 'Equivalents' is largely based on long established commercial usage, the commercially used name being recommended. It is more for convenience than botanical accuracy and is in no way a 'set of rules' to be followed by everyone. It is largely up to the individual whether he chooses to be guided by the listing or chooses to adopt the botanically correct name if this differs from the listing.

When a new species (or a new variety) of a plant is validly published it must contain a description, in Latin, for the benefit of the botanical world as a whole. However, most orchid taxonomists in the English speaking world usually follow this with a description in English. Several abbreviations may be used and the meaning of these is not always readily available so are given here.

Nomen novum (nom.nov.) a new name, i.e. a name not previously published or substituted for one in general use but found to be unacceptable.

Nomen nudum (nom. nud.) a naked name, i.e. a plant name only published without any description or figure and which cannot be allocated beyond doubt to any plant or plant group. *Nomina nuda* are rejected and illegitimate.

The symbol '!' in the introduction to a citation of the plant, i.e. its name and description. The use of this symbol indicates that the person describing the plant has seen and examined the specimen rather than relying on second-hand information.

Perhaps the best method of explaining citations is to quote a few of these.

1. *Coelogyne swaniana* Rolfe, Kew Bull. 1894 183 Bot. Mag. t7602 Syn: *C. quadrangularis* Ridl J.L.S. 32:323 1896.
The name *C. swaniana* named and described by Rolfe in the Kew Bulletin of 1894 clearly takes priority over *C. quadrangularis* named and described by Ridley in the Journal of the Linnean Society Vol. 32 page 323 of 1896. *C. quadrangularis* is a synonym and given for information only and should not be used.

2. *Encyclia lancifolia* (Lindley) Dressler and Pollard, Phytologia 21: 437, 1971.
This was named by Lindley in 1831 as *Epidendrum lancifolium* but was reclassified into the genus *Encyclia* by D. and P. in 1971 the advice to the botanical world appearing in Vol. 21 of Phytologia. Note that the same specific epithet has been retain-

ed as required by the international rules but has been slightly changed to agree grammatically with the generic name.

3. *Phaius mishmensis* (Lindl) Rchb.f. in Bonpl. 5:43 1857 Basionym: *Limatodes mishmensis* (Lindl) in Lindl. & Paxt. Fl. Gard. 3:36 1852. Syn. *Phaius roseus* Rolfe in Kew Bull. 6 1893. In this case Lindley placed the plant in the genus *Limatodes* in 1852. In 1857 Heinrich Reichenbach (known as Reichenbach filius, the son of the previous Reichenbach) reclassified the plant into the genus *Phaius* retaining the specific epithet on transfer to the new genus. This is shown as a Basionym, a term used when the original epithet is retained upon transfer. The synonym now has no nomenclatural standing.

4. *Cleisostoma aspersum* (Rchb.f.) Garay, comb. nov. in Bot. M. Leaf. 23: 4 1972.
comb.nov. means *combinatio nova*, i.e. a new combination. An unpublished plant name based on a re-arrangement of a name already published. Here both *Cleisostoma* and *aspersum* had been published previously but not in this combination.

When publishing a diagnosis (description) of a new plant the taxonomist must state a nomenclatural type as truly representing that described plant. This is called a 'holotype'. As defined, a holotype is the one specimen designated by the author as the nomenclatural type. If no holotype has been designated by the author of the diagnosis, a substitute for it may be chosen. The substitute may be called either a 'lectotype' or a 'neotype' the former name taking precedence. A lectotype is a specimen selected from the original material to serve as a nomenclatural type when the holotype was not designated or is missing.

A neotype is a specimen selected to serve as a nomenclatural type if all the material on which the name of the taxon was based is missing. From this it is obvious that as long as some of the original material is available a new type or neotype cannot be designated, or if it is, it is illegitimate.

Examples of this appear in *'The Orchid Review'* for May 1976 under the authorship of Mark W. Wood.

1. *Paphiopedilum chamberlainianum* (Sander) has been reclassified to *Paphiopedilum victoria-regina* (Sander) M.W. Wood subspecies *chamberlainianum* (Sander) M.W. Wood comb.nov. The type being that collected by Micholitz in Sumatra in 1891 and lodged at the Kew Herbarium (lectotype). This was selected from what was believed to be part of the original collection and as it still exists it must be chosen as a lectotype and the selection of a figure, as stated in Orchid Digest 35: 53-55 1971, as the lectotype must be disregarded.

2. *Paphiopedilum victoria-regina* (Sander) M.W. Wood, comb.nov. the Basionym being *Cypripedium victoria-regina* Sander in Gard. Chron. Ser. 3 11: 194 (Feb 13, 1892).
As Wood could not locate any of the dried material from which Sander made his original description he has selected a neotype from herbarium sheets at Kew and consisting of scape, buds, bracts and one open flower labelled as being from Royal Botanic Gardens, Glasnevin, April 1895.

The type designation, therefore, becomes—Type: Specimen labelled 'Royal Botanic Gardens', Glasnevin, April 1895. In Kew Herbarium (neotype).

TOPIC 6. AN ELECTRONIC THERMOSTAT FOR THE GLASSHOUSE

With the gradual penetration of electronic devices into our daily life it seems appropriate that orchid growers should be able to use an electronic device for such an important function as temperature control in the glasshouse.

The device described herein was developed by the author and has been used in his glasshouse for some years in various forms and designs. With the younger members of our population becoming more conscious of, and better instructed in, electronics many growers may have a son, a nephew or a friend sufficiently accomplished in electronics to construct a simple device as described, although its design and development posed a few problems.

Notes for the User

This unit, in its basic form, uses just one temperature sensor to operate four devices to control the temperature in the glasshouse. The design allows for one heater, which is kept 'off' by high temperature and allowed to come 'on' when the temperature falls below a selected value, plus three other devices which come 'on' with rising temperature. For example two fans and an evaporative cooler or whatever you wish.

Four knobs on the front panel allow you to set-in or alter instantaneously the temperature at which the various devices function. Isolating switches are also fitted so that the four devices can be turned 'off' while temperature set up is being done. The neon indicators let you know when the device has power fed to it without the need for the device to operate. The temperature differential is about 0.2°C, i.e. the temperature difference between 'on' and 'off'. This is considerably better than most thermostats and much easier to adjust.

The temperature sensor is in a small box located in the glasshouse in a sheltered position usually about eye level but the location is your choice. It is not advisable to house the main unit in the glasshouse, a good location being in an annexe. If this is not possible it may be housed outside in a weather-proof metal box as used by the Electricity Supply Authority to house meters, switches and fuses. A few holes between the box and the glasshouse interior are necessary for cables.

If the control of four devices is insufficient for your needs the unit may be expanded very easily to provide eight control circuits, two of which may be used as over or under temperature alarms. If desired a mains failure alarm may be included to sound in your bedroom or wherever.

Warning This equipment operates from a dangerous voltage. Construction by persons other than those knowledgeable and experienced in electricity, radio or electronics is not advised. As with all electronic devices made with off-the-shelf components, some debugging is often necessary and some electronic skill is needed.

Notes for the constructor
It is recommended that the unit be built on the panel/chassis system so that all 240 volt circuits are located below chassis. By bolting the chassis to a substantial board it will be difficult for persons to come into contact with high voltage.

In the main unit, if toggle switches are used for isolation or mains switching these must be secured to a metal strip or panel. The unit itself consumes negligible power and may be run, along with fans and water solenoids from a standard power point. If a 3 kW fan heater is used this should be permanently wired into a mercury relay, e.g. Adlake type PEP-06-240 obtainable from Circuit Components Pty. Ltd., Bexley, N.S.W. 2207. The coil of this relay is powered from the mains via the heater relay in the unit. Naturally, all metal fittings and the box housing the unit should be grounded.

If eight control circuits are needed, a second 339 is added, parallel pin for pin to the original 339, a second group of 4 potentiometers is fitted to set-in the desired temperatures and so on.

The electronic section can conveniently be built on a Tandy plug-in board 276-156 with socket to suit. One board is sufficient for the circuit shown (**Fig. T6-1**).

The temperature sensor is a silicon diode the voltage drop across which changes linearly with temperature. This is connected in a bridge circuit, the lot being housed in a 'zippy box' with 'set-min' and 'set-max' controls on the front panel of this box.

This unit hangs in a wet situation so should be reasonably well sealed. The power dissipated is small and no ventilation is needed (**Fig. T6-2**).

Technical description. As the temperature varies so does the voltage drop across the diode which changes the bridge output. This signal is amplified by the 3900 and fed to comparator 339. Four potentiometers, mounted on the front panel of the main unit provide for the set-temperature voltage at the 339. When the output from the 339 exceeds the pre-set voltage, the 339 pins 1, 2, 13 and 14 go positive causing the associated BC549 to conduct which biases the BC559 'on' so energising the relays.

For heater control the low temperature required for 'heater on' gives 0 volts at pin 1 of the 339 which biases the BC 549 to 'off' and the AC 187 to 'on', so causing the relay to energise. As the temperature rises the BC 549 conducts so biasing the AC 187 to 'off' and opening the relay. The capacitors across the transistors dampen out any oscillation of the 339. This tends to delay relay response by a second or so but in practice temperature variations in the glasshouse are slow.

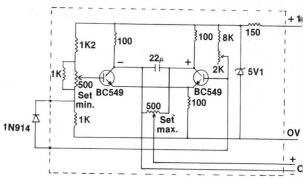

Fig. T6-2 Temperature sensor

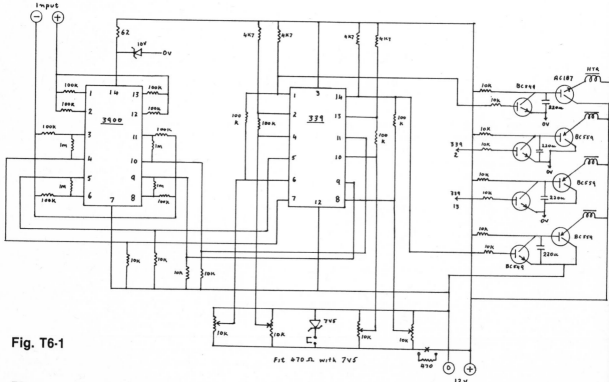

Fig. T6-1

Fit 470 Ω with 7V5

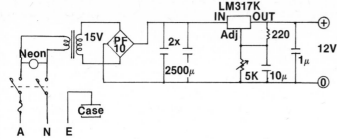

Fig. T6-3   12 v regulated power supply

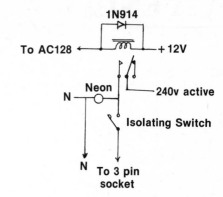

Fig. T6-4   Connections—typical relay

The Power supply, 12 volt regulated. Fig. T6-3. The transformer should have a 15 volt secondary rated at 1 amp. The PF 10 is a bridge rectifier but there are many similar types rated at 1 amp or more. The LM 317K regulator should be housed in a TO 3 heat sink and placed in a position for cooling. Adjust the 5K variable resistor for 12 volts output. Electrolytic capacitors are rated at 25 volts.

Relays. Fig. T6-4. There are several types of heavy duty relays available with a 12 volt coil in D.P.D.T. configuration. A coil resistance of some 300 ohms is satisfactory. A reverse connected diode is placed across the relay coil as protection for the transistors. Note the change of polarity when connecting across the heater relay.

Ventilation. The equipment should be placed in a ventilated cool position to limit temperature rise.

Calibration Notes. Fig. T6-5. Although the bridge should balance at 0°C there is considerable difficulty in keeping the diode constantly at this temperature so calibration of the 'set-min' control can be done at the coldest convenient minimum temperature. The temperature sensor is designed to give an output of 0.5 volts at 30°C but it is unnecessary to have exactly this temperature for calibration of the 'set-max' control. The graph shows the output voltage which should be obtained for each temperature in the range, using an 0–50°C laboratory thermometer to measure the temperature. The voltmeter should not be less than 20 000 ohms/volt. The circuit for the temperature sensor shows a 2K potentiometer in the diode feed. This allows a very fine adjustment of the output voltage at the 'set-min' temperature. This potentiometer and the 8K resistor may be replaced with a 10K resistor if a very fine adjustment is not needed and one has some patience to set the 500 ohm 'set-min' potentiometer to the desired output voltage for the low temperature adjustment. For use as a thermostat this setting is not too critical as the four front panel potentiometers allow the actual working points of the T/stat to be set in.

At the higher temperatures, say 26 or 27°C the 'set-max' control is adjusted to give the correct output voltage. The movement of one control will necessitate re-adjustment of the other, so setting up is a backward and forward shuffle between these controls.

The output polarity of the bridge circuit should be as shown on the diagram, the voltage rising with an increase in temperature.

The resistors associated with bridge balance and the 'set-min' control may need selection and small additions or variation of resistance. This circuit is sensitive to small changes in value.

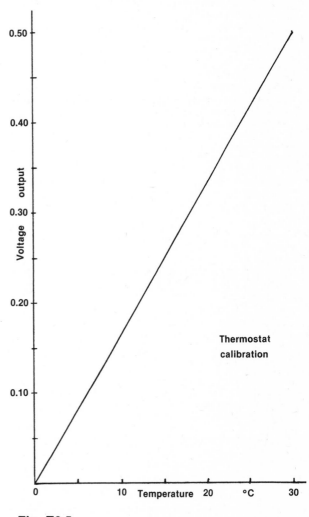

Fig. T6-5

APPENDIX 1. SUN TABLES

Horizontal and vertical angles of the sun for the stated latitudes

Date	Time a.m.	p.m.	20ºS Hor.	Vert.	27½ºS Hor.	Vert.	32½ºS Hor.	Vert.	35ºS Hor.	Vert.	37½ºS Hor.	Vert.	42½ºS Hor.	Vert.
26 May	7	5	66	7	65	3	64	1	64	0	64	0	63	0
to	8	4	58	18	57	15	55	12	55	10	55	9	55	6
19 July	10	2	37	40	34	34	32	29	32	27	31	25	30	21
	Noon		0	49	0	41	0	36	0	34	0	31	0	26
21 Mar.	7	5	85	15	83	14	82	13	81	13	81	12	80	11
and	8	4	78	28	75	26	72	25	72	25	71	24	69	22
23 Sept.	10	2	60	55	52	50	47	47	45	45	44	43	39	40
	Noon		0	70	0	63	0	57	0	55	0	53	0	48
27 Nov.	7	5	106	21	103	23	101	24	100	25	98	25	97	25
to	8	4	103	34	97	35	94	36	92	36	91	36	87	36
19 Jan.	10	2	98	62	84	62	74	60	70	60	66	60	58	58
	Noon		0	91	0	83	0	78	0	76	0	73	0	69

Notes
1. Winter and Summer angles are given from one date to another. The variations within this period are so minor as to be negligible in glasshouse design.

2. For a.m. times the horizontal bearing is east of true north. For p.m. times the horizontal bearing is west of north (see diagram).

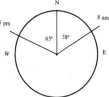

Example for Latitude 20ºS
26 May to 19 July

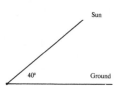

Vertical angle at 10 am and 2 pm
on 26 May to 19 July Latitude 20º S

APPENDIX 2. TECHNICAL DATA

Acidity

The element Hydrogen plays an enormously large role in life yet it is the simplest element in existence. It is best known in its molecular form (two atoms together) as a highly inflammable gas used in the past in balloons and airships. In its atomic form it consists of one proton with a positive charge and one electron with a negative charge. In biological systems it is even simpler, in that it loses the electron and becomes a proton which is represented as H^+.

Thus $H \rightarrow H^+$ plus an electron.

In biological systems the proton comes from water which under normal temperatures splits into two ions shown in steps as:

$$H_2O \rightarrow H—OH \rightarrow H + OH \rightarrow H^+ \text{and } OH^-$$

the surplus electron from the H atom becoming attached to the OH (hydroxyl ion) which now becomes negative. It has been said that 'pure' water can never really be pure as it con-

taminates itself with its own ions. A proton does not exist in water in a free state but attaches itself to another water molecule. However, this makes the understanding of acidity unnecessarily complex so here we shall consider the proton as existing alone and shown simply as H^+.

Solutions which are acidic contain a large number of H^+ and the *degree of acidity depends on the amount of H^+ in a direct ratio*. The opposite to acidity is basicity although this is more popularly known as alkalinity so we would expect an alkaline solution to have very few H^+.

From the above equation it is clear that when water ionises it splits into two ions of equal numbers and if, for some reason and by some method, we increase the number of H^+ the number of OH^- must decrease.

The product of the H^+ and OH^- ion concentration in water solutions at 25°C is 10^{-14} irrespective of where these ions come from.

In pure water or water containing a non-acidic or non-basic salt (say sodium chloride), which contributes neither H^+ nor OH^- ions then $H^+ = OH^- = 10^{-7}$ and the solution is neutral.

If an acid is added to the water H^+ becomes greater than OH^-.

Suppose the concentration of H^+ increases 10 times, then $H^+ = 10^{-6}$ and $OH^- = 10^{-8}$ so the product of the concentrations continue to $= 10^{-14}$ but as 10^{-6} is greater than 10^{-7} (10 times greater) the solution is more acid.

The above is the basis of the pH scale which goes from 0 (highly acid) to 14 (highly alkaline) with neutrality at pH 7 where H^+ and OH^- balance.

Why pH? The H is the symbol for Hydrogen the importance of which is given above. The small 'p' is attributed to the Latin word for 'pondus' meaning weight. So pH reads as the weight of Hydrogen which is a true representation of the term. pH may be defined as 'the negative common logarithm of the H^+ concentration in gram ions/litre'. The term 'gram ions' is a measure of weight.

The symbol 'p' has since been used to mean 'the common logarithm of' and may be encountered in other measurements not of concern here.

The useful pH range to the plantsman is 5 to 8. As the range is derived from a common logarithm, pH 5 is 10 times more acid than pH 6 and 100 times more acid than pH 7. The figures appear to be going the wrong way because it is a negative logarithm and 10^{-5} is greater in value than 10^{-6}.

Practically pH can be measured with pH meters which vary a great deal in cost. Fortunately high accuracy is not needed for horticultural work and the cheaper versions are usually satisfactory. Another method is to use an indicator dye which changes colour with a change of pH. If this is purchased it should cover only a restricted range, as explained above, otherwise a lot of scale is useless. The colour of the dye is compared with a colour scale on the bottle and read off as pH.

So by definition it is incorrect to talk about the pH of soil, of bark or of a bench. What really concerns us is the amount of hydrogen ions passed into water surrounding these solid objects.

In a pot, full of bark and plant roots each piece of bark and root is surrounded by a film of water. Hydrogen ions have been contributed to this water film by both the bark and the roots so how do we measure the pH of this water? Certainly not by taking out a few pieces of bark and placing them in a large cup of water and then measuring the pH of the water in the cup. The hydrogen ions in the water film of the bark have been grossly diluted by the water in the cup. Similarly it is useless taking a few pieces of bark from the bulk supply, tossing these into a cup of distilled water and attempting to measure the pH. The amount of dilution is important and there are various standards adopted by measuring authorities. A useful one for soil is to add distilled water amounting to 2½ times the soil volume. This gives sufficient liquid to make the measurement but not enough to cause gross dilution. A standard for solid insoluble lumps like bark does not appear to exist so readers may safely use as little water as possible to make a measurement.

For a potful of bark and plant the soundest method may be to collect a little drainage water from the pot and measure this. It does not really matter whether the tap water was neutral, acid or alkaline it is the final result that matters. If the solution is not sufficiently acid the addition of citric acid (about 200 to 300 milligrams per litre of water) will provide more hydrogen ions and the citric acid, being a natural plant acid, is not likely to harm the plant or the user. To make the potting substrate less acid, place some dolomite on to the surface of the substrate and water in.

The measurement of pH can vary widely even over a few days, if the solution being measured is poorly buffered. Buffering is the ability of a solution to resist change in acidity. The soil solution in sandy soils is very poorly buffered whereas a soil rich in organic matter is highly buffered. The latter requires a lot of say, dolomite, to reduce its acidity whereas only a small amount of dolomite is needed to reduce the acidity of a sandy soil solution by the same amount. This can be used as a guide but one would think that the more the bark breaks down into finer particles the better its buffering capacity.

Multiples and submultiples—prefixes and abbreviations as used in the SI system (*Systeme International d'Unites*), the Metric System.

10^{12}	tera	T	Note use of upper case for the abbreviation and lower case for prefix.
10^9	giga	G	
10^6	mega	M	
10^3	kilo	k	
10^2	hecto	h	
10	deca	da	
10^{-1}	deci	d	
10^{-2}	centi	c	
10^{-3}	milli	m	
10^{-6}	micro	μ	
10^{-9}	nano	n	
10^{-12}	pico	p	

A millimetre (mm) is part of a metre and a nanometer (nm) is 1000th million (10^{-9}) part of a metre. This latter term is used to measure the wavelengths of light. Micrometres (μm) are used frequently to indicate the size of fungal spores or bacteria. The Angstrom is sometimes referred to in older publications. 10 A = 1 nm so $1A = 10^{-10}$ metres.

Temperature conversion

Degrees Celsius and Degrees Fahrenheit. $1°C = 1.8°F$.

so $20°C = (20 \times 1.8) + 32 = 68°F$

and $77°F = \dfrac{(77 - 32)}{1.8} = \dfrac{45}{1.8} = 25°C$

for Degrees Kelvin add 273 to the °C figure.

$20°C + 273 = 293°K$

Caution

A rather silly error is often seen in texts which have not been properly checked and edited, in respect of temperature.

For example, it is often stated that the night temperature should be 5°C (41°F) cooler than day temperature. This has been arrived at, no doubt, by applying the formula rigidly as
$°F = °C \times 9/5 + 32$ so $5°C \times 9/5 + 32 = 41°F$
and so it does in absolute values but not in a difference sense where it equals 9°F.

For example 20°C day temperature $= 68°F$ and 5°C cooler is 15°C night temperature $= 59°F$—difference 9°F.

Relative Humidity measurement using wet and dry bulb thermometers

For horticultural purposes it is seldom necessary to know the R.H. with a high degree of accuracy; within a few percent is sufficient so the following table is a simplified version.

Dry Bulb °C	Wet bulb difference °C									
	0.5	1	1.5	2	2.5	3	3.5	4	4.5	5
13/14/15	95	90	84	79	74	70	65	60	56	51
16/17/18	95	90	86	81	77	72	68	64	59	55
19/20/21	96	91	87	83	78	74	70	66	62	59
22/23/24	96	92	88	84	80	76	72	69	65	62
25/26/27	96	92	88	85	81	78	74	71	67	64
28/29/30	96	93	89	86	82	79	76	72	69	66

APPENDIX 3.   FURTHER READING

Australian

1. *Australian Orchid Review.* A quarterly periodical available by subscription within Australia for $11 p.a. (1982) from Australian Orchid Review, 14 McGill St., Lewisham, N.S.W. 2049.

This is a general interest publication having a total of near 300 pages for the four 1981 issues including advertising. Every Australian orchid enthusiast should subscribe if only for the sole purpose of knowing what is going on, what is planned in the orchid scene and what can be obtained from where. The advertisements are quite useful in this respect. The journal is the official organ of the various State Orchid Societies throughout Australia.

2. *The Orchadian.* This is the journal of the Australasian Native Orchid Society (A.N.O.S.) published quarterly by A.N.O.S., Box C106, P.O. Clarence St., Sydney, N.S.W. 2000. The cost (1982) is $10 p.a. which covers four issues of the journal and annual membership to A.N.O.S.

A volume of 12 issues contains some 290 pages. This journal is dedicated to the study and care of Australasian indigenous orchids. Note that 'Australasian' includes New Zealand and New Guinea. This is a high class journal vital to all those having an interest in orchids of the above region. Many of the articles attempt to sort out some of the classification and nomenclature problems of Australian orchids plus descriptions of new species from both Australia and New Guinea. It is well illustrated by line drawings and black and white photographs but no colour. Highly recommended, not only to Australian native orchid buffs, but to all those persons having an interest in species, their identification and culture.

United States of America

3. *Orchid Digest.* This is published by the Orchid Digest Corporation, C/- Mrs N.H. Atkinson, P.O. Box 916, Carmichael, California, 95608, U.S.A. The cost (1982) is US$16 for six issues at two monthly intervals.

This is, without doubt, an outstanding periodical with maximum colour illustrations and minimal advertising. The 1980 issue had a total of 238 pages but these measure 28 cm × 21 cm. For the species enthusiast and plant geographer it is an indipensable periodical but the more parochial orchid growers may not find the material of interest. It is primarily a journal of plants, not of shows, awards, societies or personalities.

4. *American Orchid Society Bulletin.* This is published monthly by the American Orchid Society, 84 Sherman St., Cambridge, Massachusetts 02140, U.S.A. The subscription is US$20 p.a. which also gives membership to the A.O.S.

Each issue has about 130 pages 23 cm × 15 cm but half of each issue is advertising which may not be of great interest to Australian readers. Some very good material is contained in this journal with a large number of colour plates. Both species and hybrids are covered plus much information on culture. Material is contributed from authors throughout the world so the content is not excessively American. This is a journal needed by all orchid growers anxious to keep up with world conditions and views rather than just their local doings.

United Kingdom

The Orchid Review, sometimes called the English Orchid Review in Australia to differentiate it from our own O.R., is published by The Orchid Review Ltd. 5 Orchid Ave., Kingsteignton, Newton Abbot, Devon TQ12 3HG, England. In 1980 eight issues cost $8.50 but there are now 12 issues p.a.

A small journal of some 27 pages dealing with cultural conditions in England, awards to plants at shows, with a few articles of general interest. This journal is known mainly for its listing of new orchid hybrids a subject of interest to those breeding new hybrids. There is a modest amount of advertising of little use to Australian readers.

Books

Of these there are many, mainly of the 'Flora' type, e.g. *Native Orchids of Taiwan.* Book lists are available from the addresses given herein. Very few of the more technical and botanical books are available in Australia. One local book must be mentioned. This is *Australian Indigenous Orchids* by A.W. Dockrill which is a necessity for all interested in this subject. It is published by The Society for Growing Australian Plants, 860 Henry Lawson Drive, Picnic Point, N.S.W. 2213 and is not sold by booksellers. A large volume dealing mainly with Australian epiphytic orchids and containing line drawings, technical descriptions and habitats. A great reference book.

Other publications mentioned in Chapter 7

1. *Handbook on Orchid Nomenclature and Registration* published by the International Orchid Commission and available from the Royal Horticultural Society at the address given in Chapter 7.

2. *Sanders Hybrid Lists.* Members of the American Orchid Society may obtain these from the Society or otherwise from 'Mary Noble McQuerry Orchid Books' at the address given in this Appendix. Write for a quotation. The listing commences in 1946 but reprints have been made so they are not rare books.

Overseas book suppliers

Twin Oaks Books, 4343 Causeway Dr., Lowell, Michigan 49331, U.S.A.

Mary Noble McQuerry Orchid Books, 5700 W. Salerno Rd., Jacksonville, Florida 32210, U.S.A.

Wheldon & Wesley Ltd., Lytton Lodge, Codicote, Hitchin, Herts SG4 8TE, U.K.

APPENDIX 4. GLOSSARY

Abscission. The falling off of leaves or flowers usually at an abscission layer of easily broken cells.

Agar. A substance derived from seaweed and used to form a gel in otherwise liquid mixtures.

Angiosperm. A vascular plant bearing seeds in a case (ovary).

Anther. The part of a flower which produces pollen.

Anthesis. The opening of the flowers or the flowering period.

Anthocyanin. A water soluble colouring substance giving flowers the red, mauve, purple colours.

Asexual. Meaning not sexual, being vegetative or from non-sex or body (somatic) cells.

Asymbiotic. Refers to the germination of orchid seed without fungus. Not symbiotic.

Autotrophic. Able to manufacture its own food from energy and simple materials.

Axillary. Formed in the angle between leaf and stem.

Backbulb. Refers to sympodial orchids where a pseudobulb has matured and lost its leaves.

Bifoliate. Having two leaves usually at the top of one pseudobulb.

Bigeneric. Applied to hybrids from parents of two genera.

Bract. A small leaflike tissue at the base of a stem or flower.

Callus. A fleshy growth on the lip.

Cambium. A layer of cells between xylem and phloem which annually expands the stem diameter. Not in orchids.

Capsule. A dry, dehiscent fruit as in an orchid.

Carotene. A non-water soluble colouring substance in the chloroplasts. Assists in photosynthesis and often gives yellow colouring to leaves.

Caudicle. A stalk, in orchids used to attach pollinia to stipe.

Chloroplast. An organelle containing chlorophyll (and many other substances) which is located in the cytoplasm.

Chlorophyll. A complex organic molecule absorbing radiant energy in the 'red' and 'blue' parts of the visible spectrum.

Clone. A single plant raised from a seed plus all of its subsequent progeny derived from vegetative propagation.

Column. An organ in an orchid flower formed by the union of stamens and pistils with their supporting tissue.

Column Foot. This is an extension of the base of the column, not always occurring, to which the lip is attached.

Cultivar. An individual plant and those plants derived from it by vegetative propagation. Not to be confused with a variety.

Disc. The upper part of the middle section of the lip.

DNA. De-oxyribonucleic acid. Prominent in chromosomes where it provides the supporting structure for the genes.

Dorsal. The back or outer surface of an organ. Also used to indicate the upper sepal of a flower.

Endemic. Native to a region and not found elsewhere.

Enzymes. Proteins which carry out specific functions within an organism as distinct from structural proteins.

Epiphyte. A plant which grows on another using it as a support only and is not a parasite.

Exotic. Not native. Coming from another country.

Family. A major subdivision in the Plant Kingdom commonly including many related genera.

Fertilisation. The fusion of two sex cells (gametes) to form a new individual. In plants this may follow pollination. Fertilisation results in the formation of a fruit and seeds.

Fruit. The seed bearing part of the plant.

Gamete. A sex cell contained in either the pollen or the ovule.

Genotype. The hereditary characteristics transmitted from a parent to its progeny.

Genus. A taxonomic category above species but below the level of family, tribe and sub-tribe. The generic name forms the first word in the botanical name of the plant.

Geophyte. A plant which grows in the ground as distinct from an epiphyte.

Hyphae. Individual filaments of fungal growth. (sing. hypha)

Inferior ovary. Said of the ovary when it is below the flower parts.

Inflorescence. The flower or flower cluster of a plant borne on a scape. There may be more than one inflorescence on a plant at the same time.

Internode. The space between nodes on a stem at which point leaves arise or between pseudobulbs on a rhizome.

Keiki. (pron. kay-kee) An offshoot arising from the stem of a plant.

Labellum. The correct name for the lip of an orchid flower.

Megayear. One million years.

Mycelium. Refers to the filamentous growth of a fungus. See also Hyphae.

Node. A joint on a stem or pseudobulb from which a leaf or bract arises singly or multiple.

Nucleus. The major organelle of a cell containing the genetic material.

Osmosis. The diffusion of a liquid (water in plants) through a membrane to dilute a salt concentration within that membrane. Ex-osmosis is the flow from the plant into the substrate. This is still osmosis but in the reverse direction to that needed by the plant.

Ovule. An embryonic seed encased in the ovary and bearing a gamete which is fertilised by the pollen gamete.

Phenolic. A substance, of which there are many, formed from a 6-carbon ring compound called phenol. Many plant acids and anthocyanins are regarded as phenolic compounds.

Phenotype. The observable characteristics of a plant due to varying environmental conditions even though the genotype may be identical to others of the species.

Respiration. The process by which cells use up food and produce energy. Water and carbon dioxide are produced as by-products.

Resupinate. The turning of the flower, in bud, so that the lip is 'down'. Many orchids do not resupinate leaving the lip pointing upwards on the open flower.

Rhizome. A horizontal stem prominent in sympodial growth and composed of the bases of successive shoots.

Staminode. A sterile stamen. Usually used to describe the disc shape structure at the top of the column of a *Paphiopedilum*.

Stigma. A part of the flower. The part of the column in the orchid, which is receptive to the pollinia and frequently provides food for pollen tube growth.

Synsepalum. This is a ventral or lower sepal produced by the joining together edgewise of two lateral sepals. Prominent in the *Paphiopedilum* and related genera.

Terete. Circular in cross section. Often used to describe 'round' leaves.

Tesselate. Arranged in a mosaic pattern as in some leaves.

Transpiration. The evaporation of water through the stomata.

Variety. A plant population having minor differences from the type species. To be used only in respect of species never for hybrids. For hybrids use cultivar.

Whorl. A circle of three or more leaves, or flower parts attached at the same level on a stem.

INDEX

Subjects listed in the Contents and List of Plates are not included in this Index.

Acidity, 76
Alkaloids, 5
Anther cap, 2, 21, 53
Anthocyanins, 70
Apostasioideae, 6, 12, 21
Asexual, 52, 54
ATP, 70, 71
Autogamous, 6

Bacterial disease, 22, 59
Birds, 5
Breeding, plant, 30, 53
Buffering, 77
Bulbophyllum globuliforme, 6
Bulbophyllum minutissimum, 6

C_3, 70, 71
C_4, 28, 70, 71
CAM, 29, 70, 71
Capsule, 8, 53, 54
Carbon di-oxide, 22, 23, 29, 65, 69, 71
Caudicle, 22
Cell, 19, 69
Cellulose, 19, 25
Chlorophyll, 6, 69, 70
Chloroplast, 69, 70
Chromosomes, 7, 23, 59
CITES, 10
Climate, 14, 16
Codes, 30, 67, 72
Column, 21, 53
Community pots, 56, 57
Combinatio nova, 73
Conservation, 10
Cooling glasshouse, 28, 29, 64, 65
Cork, 24, 51, 55
Cultivars, 31, 54
Culture, 15, 60
Cyanobacteria, 19, 69
Cypripedioideae, 6, 12, 21
Cypripedium, 8

Deficiency, nutrient, 61
Deflasking, 56
Diagnosis, 72
Dicotyledons, 11
Disc, viscid, 6, 21, 22, 53
DNA, 8, 59

Ecology, 7, 70, 71
Electromagnetic radiation, 25, 26, 27, 62
Endodermis, 20
Energy, 25, 27, 28, 69
Enzymes, 69, 70
Epidendroideae, 12
Epiphytes, 4, 8, 9, 20, 24, 54
Epithets, 30
Evaporative cooler, 28, 65
Exodermis, 20
Ex-osmosis, 61

Family, 11, 12, 13
Fans, 18, 28, 29, 64, 65
Fertilisers, 19, 22, 24, 25, 29, 55, 56
Fibreglass, 16, 18
Flower, 6, 11, 12, 13, 14, 21
Flower colour, 13, 70
Flower induction, 28
Form, 13
Fruits, 11, 53, 54
Fungi, 15, 52, 67, 68

Generic/Genera, 12, 13, 30, 53, 72
Genes, 23, 59, 69
Genotype, 7
Geophytes, 4, 20, 24, 54, 68, 71
Germination, 8, 52, 68
Glasshouse, 17, 18, 62
Glasshouse floor, 62
Grex epithet, 31, 32

Half wall house, 62
Hawaian Islands, 5
Heat loss, 18, 62, 63, 64
Heat storage, 17, 18, 63, 64
Heating, 62, 63, 64
Holotype, 73
Housing, 16, 62
Humidity, 9, 16, 17, 25, 26, 28, 57, 65, 71, 77
Hybrids, 14, 30, 31, 32, 53
Hydrogen, 70, 76, 77

Illegitimate, 72, 73
Indicator dyes, 77
Inflorescence, 20
Infra-red radiation, 27
Insects, 7, 9, 15
Instrumentation, 65
Intergeneric hybrids, 31
International Registration Authority, 30, 31

Jewel orchids, 23, 25
Journals, 2, 72, 78

Keikis, 55
Keratins, 5
Knudson, 52
Krakatao, 5, 68

Leaching, 9, 68
Leaves, 6, 22, 71
Lectotype, 73
Lichens, 8
Light, 8, 9, 23, 25, 28, 62, 63, 70, 71
Lignin, 25
Litter, 68

Magnesium, 70
Malesia, 4
Malic acid, 71
Manganese, 70
Meiosis, 23
Mericlones, 14, 15, 55
Microclimates, 16
Minerals, 23
Mitosis, 23
Monocotyledons, 11, 21
Monopodial, 20, 55
Multiples & Sub-multiples, 77
Mycelium, 67, 68
Mycorrhiza, 5, 67, 68

NADP, 70
Neotype, 73
Nomen novum, 72
Nomen nudem, 72
Nomina generica conservanda, 72
Nutrients, 6, 8, 20, 61

Offshoots, 31, 55
Orchidaceae, 11, 72
Orchidoideae, 12
Ovary, 12, 21, 53

Panicle, 21
Pasteurising, 56
Pedicel, 21
Peduncle, 21
Pests, 56, 58, 67
Petals, 21
pH, 77
Phenolics, 5, 8, 68
Phenotype, 7, 8
Pheromone, 7
Phloem, 20
Photosynthesis, 6, 16, 25, 28, 52, 69, 71
Phyte, 4
Phytoalexins, 68
Phytophthera, 59
Pith, 20
Plasmalemma, 19

Plasmolysis, 19, 61
Plastic, 17
Ploidy, 23
Pollen storage, 54
Pollination, 6, 7, 9, 52, 53
Pollinia, 2, 6, 7, 12, 21, 22, 53
Propagation, 52
Protoembryo, 8, 68
Pseudobulb, 20, 54, 55
Pseudocopulation, 7
Pseudomonas aeruginosa, 60
Ptyophagy, 68
Purchasing orchids, 14
Pythium, 59

Raceme, 21, 54
Rachis, 21
Radiation, 25, 26, 27, 28, 62
Rainfall, 9, 70
Registering hybrids, 30
Respiration, 16, 17, 25, 28, 71
Rhizoctonia, 68
Roadbase, 17, 62
Roots, 15, 19, 20, 54, 55
RUDP, 70, 71

Salting up, 19, 61
Saprophytes, 6, 9, 68
Scape, 21
Section, 12
Seed, 5, 8, 52, 53, 68
Sepals, 21
Sexual, 52
Shadehouse, 16, 17
Siting, 16, 17
Sky dome, 62
Solar energy, 62, 64
Solar glasshouses, 62
Species, 7, 12, 13, 30, 72
Spiranthoideae, 12
Stele, 20
Stigma, 2, 6, 7, 21, 53
Stipe, 21, 22
Stomates, 22, 26, 71
Sub-family, 12, 13
Sub-species, 13
Sub-tribe, 12, 72
Substrates, 4, 19, 24, 56
Sugars, 6, 7, 20, 52, 67, 70
Sun angles, 16, 76
Sun flecks, 27
Sympodial, 20, 54

Temperature, 9, 16, 23, 28, 29, 63, 64, 73, 77
Tissue propagation, 55
Tolypophagy, 68
Tonoplast, 19
Transpiration, 26
Tribe, 12, 13, 72
Tuber, 20
Tuberoid, 20
Turgor, 19

Ultra violet radiation, 26, 27
Underground orchids, 6

Vacuole, 19, 71
Variety, 13, 72
Varietal name, 31
Velamen, 9, 19
Ventilation, 26, 29, 64, 65, 71
Virus, 60
Visible light, 25, 27, 28

Water, 8, 9, 19, 22, 23, 25, 26, 28, 55, 60, 70
Wax, 22
Weldmesh, 17, 51
Whorls, 21
Wind, 17, 29, 64, 65

Xylem, 20